THE SOUTH AFRICAN LITURGY

THE
SOUTH AFRICAN LITURGY

THE STORY OF
THE REVISION OF THE RITE AND
ITS CONSECRATION PRAYER

BY PETER HINCHLIFF

SUBWARDEN OF ST. PAUL'S COLLEGE
GRAHAMSTOWN

CAPE TOWN
OXFORD UNIVERSITY PRESS
1959

Oxford University Press, Amen House, London E.C.4

GLASGOW   NEW YORK   TORONTO   MELBOURNE   WELLINGTON
BOMBAY   CALCUTTA   MADRAS   KARACHI   KUALA LUMPUR
CAPE TOWN   IBADAN   NAIROBI   ACCRA

PRINTED IN THE UNION OF SOUTH AFRICA BY
THE RUSTICA PRESS, PTY., LTD., WYNBERG, CAPE

FOR
CONSTANCE HINCHLIFF
AND
CONSTANCE BAZELEY

CONTENTS

ABBREVIATIONS

The following abbreviations are used in the text:

Alternative Form—*An Alternative Form of the Order for the Administration of the Holy Communion* (various editions, 1919-24)

A.C. VIII—*The Apostolic Constitutions*, Book VIII

Considerations—*Considerations bearing on the Petition to the Episcopal Synod, addressed to the Lord Bishop of Natal*

Constitution and Canons—*The Constitution and Canons of the Church of the Province of South Africa* (various editions, 1870-1950)

C.Q.R.—*Church Quarterly Review*

Historical Records—*The Historical Records of the Church of the Province of South Africa*, compiled by C. Lewis and G. E. Edwards (S.P.C.K., 1934)

Proposals—*Proposals for the Revision of the Anaphora*, by J. S. Bazeley and C. J. B. Gould (Grahamstown, 1913)

Proposed Form—*The Proposed Form of the South African Liturgy* (1918)

N.B. The editions of the South African rite are referred to by date of publication, which is usually, but not always, the year following that in which the edition was approved by episcopal synod.

ACKNOWLEDGEMENTS

TO RHODES University, Grahamstown, for permission to adapt this book from a thesis originally submitted for the degree of doctor of philosophy in that university.

To the episcopal synod of the Province of South Africa for permission to quote from the Prayer Book; and to the Lord Bishop of Grahamstown, chairman of the liturgical committee, for permission to use the official records.

To the late Archbishop of Cape Town for permission to consult the records and minutes of episcopal synod kept at Bishopscourt; and to the present Archbishop for confirming that permission.

To the Rev. W. D. Maxwell, Professor of Divinity at Rhodes University, who supervised the original work, and to the Rev. Canon N. Blamires, Warden of St. Paul's College, Grahamstown, for continued encouragement and advice; and to the Rev. Canon E. C. Ratcliffe, Regius Professor of Divinity at Cambridge, for many helpful suggestions and criticisms.

To Mrs. C. J. B. Gould and the Rev. K. E. Driver, who gave me a large number of books and some very valuable letters which had belonged to the Rev. Canon Gould, for St. Paul's College library and to be used in preparing this work.

To Mrs. J. S. Bazeley, who similarly gave me valuable letters and papers which had belonged to the Rev. J. S. Bazeley, to be kept in the College library and used for this work.

To the authors and publishers who have kindly allowed me to quote from their works, and particularly to the Rev. R. C. D. Jasper and the Rev. A. Pierce Jones.

To the Rt. Rev. L. N. Fisher, the Rt. Rev. the Lord Bishop of Kimberley and Kuruman, the Ven. H. E. Wraige, Fr. Bernard Horner, C.R., Fr. Christopher Millington, C.R., the Rev. G. Bacon, the Rev. C. E. Earle Bulwer, and H. M. Matthew, Esq., Secretary to the Diocese of Grahamstown, who lent me material for use in preparing this book; and to the many others who gave me valuable information which I could not otherwise have obtained.

To the Trustees of the Crewe Trust, Mrs. J. S. Bazeley, E. L. Whitehead, Esq., and the Provincial Publications Board, whose generous assistance has made publication possible.

To the students of St. Paul's College, who patiently accepted my attempts in lectures to assemble and arrange the material which has gone into this work; to several of them in particular —the Rev. T. D. Verryn, the Rev. R. R. Snyman, and the Rev. D. St. J. White—who helped to check references and to verify sources; and to Mr. Peter Barendsen for making the index.

CHAPTER ONE

THE PRELIMINARY MOVES

THE BOOK of Common Prayer came to this country as a part of the establishment of a British administration at the Cape. Initially, the Dutch Reformed Church was guaranteed, by treaty, the rights and privileges of the official Church of the country. The position of the Anglican Church was uncertain. There was a sense in which it was 'established', but this was primarily in the sense that it was regarded as an integral part of the Church of England as by law established, in England. It took three major law-suits, and a vast tangle of subsidiary litigation, before the position was made clear. The first of these suits concerned the right of the bishop of Cape Town to summon the clergy to synod. This was the case of *Long* v. *The Bishop of Cape Town*. The second, *In re the Bishop of Natal*, concerned the rights of the bishop of Cape Town as metropolitan, and was part of the long Colenso controversy. The third, *Merriman* v. *Williams*, was in a sense a consequence of the same controversy, and concerned the Church's right to hold property. Without synods, metropolitan, or property, the Church could hardly exist in the colony at all except as either a department of the colonial administration or an extension of the Province of Canterbury.

The third suit, *Merriman* v. *Williams*, resulted in both the colonial courts and the Privy Council declaring that in law the Anglican Church in this country was severed 'root and branch' from the established Church of England. Such a judgment could not, of course, affect the spiritual union between the two, but it did, in spite of the undeniable incidental hardships to which it exposed the Church, declare that the Church was free from the bonds of establishment. One might have supposed that this left the Church free to do as it liked with the Prayer Book, also, but, in fact, provincial synod had 'received' the Book of Common Prayer as a part of the constitution adopted in 1870. The Book was recognized as one of the standards of faith, and the synod disclaimed for itself the right to alter such standards. The synod had, at the same time, laid down in Article X of the constitution that liturgical revision might be undertaken in the Province provided that nothing was done contrary to the spirit and teaching of the Book of Common Prayer. These apparently conflicting provisions have resulted, in effect, in the publication of a revised Prayer Book to be used as an alternative to and not as a substitute for the Book of 1662.

The bishops, moreover, when they first issued the alternative communion office, sought legal advice, wanting to be assured that they had the power, under the constitution, to revise the Book of Common Prayer at all. Obviously the unpleasantness and distress which had marked the discovery of the fact of disestablishment had made the bishops wary of doing anything which might further weaken the links between the province and the Church of England. Twice, indeed, in the twenty years following the *Merriman* case, attempts were made to repeal the famous 'third proviso' of the South African Constitution. This proviso had the effect of asserting that the judgments of the Privy Council were not binding on the Church of the Province, and it was the third proviso which had led the judges in the *Merriman* case to maintain that the Church of the Province and the Church of England were legally two entirely separate and different bodies.

In each attempt to repeal the proviso it was asserted that such repeal would strengthen the bonds between the two churches. On the second occasion it was also argued that it would help to heal the schism caused by the Colenso controversy. In neither case was the attempt successful, but it is clear that as late as fifty years ago the question of this relationship between the province and the Church 'at home' was very much a live issue. There were many who felt that there ought to be a legal as well as a spiritual connexion. Indeed, a schism with its roots in this very question continues among Anglicans in this country to the present time. It must be remembered, moreover, that the first Lambeth conference was not held until 1867. Even in the next decade or two after that, the 'Anglican Communion' must have been an unfamiliar idea; a union based on tenuous and untested bonds.

Of all the links which remained to bind the province to the 'Mother Church' in England after 1880, the Prayer Book must have seemed to be the most real and the most obvious. When, for instance, the legislature of the colony of Natal was asked in 1910 to pass the Church Properties Act, another step towards the healing of the Colensoite schism, the Book of 1662 was quite clearly regarded as a guarantee of the 'Anglicanism' of the Church of the Province. The Act provided that in services conducted in buildings which had once belonged to the 'Church of England' and which might join the Church of the Province, nothing might be required which was not required in the services of the Church of England. In 1924, when provincial synod agreed on the final form of the eucharistic liturgy, synod desired to affirm

its continued loyalty to the Order for the Administration of the Lord's Supper in the Book of Common Prayer, and to its use, where retained, as a sufficient and completely catholic rite, endeared to millions of churchmen by the most sacred associations.[1]

Even before this, episcopal synod had, in 1911 and again in 1915, passed resolutions aimed at securing, as far as was within the power of the bishops of a single province, some measure of uniformity in matters of revision within the whole Anglican Communion. Prima facie, one would expect to find the authorities reluctant to initiate any revision.

Yet there were compelling reasons for revision. It was 'in the air'. The constitution of 1870 had made provision for it, though it had not laid down any specific machinery to be used.[2] Resolutions of the Lambeth conference of 1867 had laid down the conditions that it was desirable for provinces to observe in revising the Prayer Book. Such revision, it was held, ought not to deviate from the doctrinal position of the 1662 book and ought to have due regard to the use of the book in the Anglican Communion as a whole. Subsequent conferences affirmed the right of provinces to revise the book and were willing to allow a certain measure of elasticity in Anglican worship. In England there was a similar desire for revision, resulting in the Letters of Business issued to the Convocations in 1906.

At first in South Africa the process was very slow. Such revision as was attempted in the provincial synod of 1870 was concerned only with adapting those parts of the 1662 book which obviously could not be used in South Africa, as they stood.[3] The only change made in the eucharistic liturgy was far from startling. It was

---

[1] *Constitution and Canons* (1939), p. 121 (Act 19, sec. 3).
[2] *Constitution and Canons* (1870), Article X.
[3] *Constitution and Canons* (1870), pp. 44 ff., repeated in *Constitution and Canons* (1939), pp. 160 ff. The subsequent, and most recent, edition (1950) no longer contains them since the publication of the final South African Prayer Book.

agreed that the Longer Exhortation might be omitted on all except four occasions in the year. Certain provision was also made for clergymen working in the diocese of Bloemfontein (in the Republic of the Orange Free State) to omit references to the Queen from the prayers. But the missionary responsibilities of the Church, alone, would have made revision essential. Something far more extensive in adapting the Book of Common Prayer to the practical political and social conditions of South Africa was inevitable. Slowly, reluctantly even, men ceased to regard the Prayer Book as possessing any verbal infallibility, and the first few hesitant steps towards revision were taken. At first these hardly affected the liturgy at all. In 1900 the celebrant was given permission to use both of the prayers, which in 1662 are alternatives, after the communion. In 1911 systematic revision was begun.

By this time, of course, the English Convocations had received their Letters of Business of 1906, and in that very year the English archbishops appointed an Advisory Committee on Liturgical Questions.[4] It must have seemed to the South African bishops that they were moving ahead, slowly and comfortably, hand in hand with their brethren 'at home'.

In 1911 episcopal synod issued a schedule of permitted modifications of and additions to the 1662 book. These are printed, but not in schedule form, in *Constitution and Canons* (1939), on pages 160 ff. The original schedule was entitled 'Suggestions and Adaptations of Services'. Here earlier changes allowed by provincial and episcopal synods were brought together with certain new modifications, and issued on the authority of the bishops. The bishop of Pretoria, for instance, sent out with the schedule of 1911 a pastoral letter *Ad Clerum* containing detailed suggestions as to the actual conduct of services; but these referred to ceremonial and devotional rather than to liturgical matters. As far as the eucharist was concerned, the 1911 schedule permitted the omission of the Decalogue and of the prayer for the King, provided that they were read once on Sundays. The form of administration might be shortened, provided that it was used once in its entirety. Certain additional collects, epistles, and gospels were provided, and there was also a scheme for combining matins, litany, and the eucharist in one Sunday morning service. This last provision directed that matins should begin with 'O Lord, open thou our

[4] R. C. D. Jasper, *Walter Howard Frere* (Alcuin Club, 1954), p. 26.

lips', and continue to the *Benedictus* immediately followed by the second and third collects. Then came a hymn and the litany up to the *Kyries*, the prayer of St. Chrysostom, the collect, epistle, and gospel for the day, and the rest of the 1662 liturgy.

The bishops' scheme for combining and shortening the three morning services is of particular interest because it follows exactly the pattern suggested by Dr. W. H. Frere, C.R., later bishop of Truro, in *Some Principles of Liturgical Reform* (pages 157 ff.). Frere was anxious that one result of revision in England should be a compressed Sunday morning service, combining the Prayer Book scheme of matins, litany, and holy communion in one rite more suited to the twentieth century.

The ideal of the [1662] Book is clear enough. Morning Prayer, followed by Litany and Communion Service, either continuously or separately, is the provision the Book makes; it is also the requirement which was actually laid upon the great churches and their clergy in the early days of the Prayer Book.

The main hindrance to the recovery of the ideal is the length of time required for the performance of the whole group of Sunday morning services in their present form.[5]

In addition to the compression of these three services, Frere desired a further rearrangement of the existing prayers of the 1662 eucharistic rite. This rearrangement placed the Comfortable Words, prayer of Humble Access, *Sursum corda*, Preface and *Sanctus*, prayer of Consecration, prayer of Oblation, and the Lord's prayer, in that order, linking the last three of these together to form a continuous canon.[6]

Frere's book was published in March 1911, and must have enjoyed a fairly wide popularity, for it had to be reprinted two months later. Episcopal synod met later in the same year to issue the schedule of permitted modifications. According to the minutes of the synod, the session was held in Pietermaritzburg on the 7th and following days of October 1911. It would surely allow too much to coincidence to suppose that two identical schemes for the compressed rite originated independently of each other in the course of the same year. The bishops differed from Frere in retaining the prayer of St. Chrysostom, which rather spoilt the liturgical purity of the compressed form. Frere used the *Kyries* of

[5] W. H. Frere, *Some Principles of Liturgical Reform* (John Murray, 1911), pp. 151, 154.
[6] Frere, pp. 191 ff.

the litany as those of the eucharist also. The only other difference was that the bishops provided for the singing of hymns. Otherwise the two schemes agreed in detail, even to the places at which the salutation 'The Lord be with you' was to be inserted. It is hard to escape the impression that the schedule of 1911 was the result of Frere's book. Even if the bishops had not seen the book as finally published, they may have been in touch with Frere while he was preparing his work for publication. We know that they certainly turned to him for help at a later date in the preparation of the form of 1919. They may have done so at this stage. The bishops' manner of dealing with the conflation of the three morning offices is the most striking evidence because it is the least likely to have been the result of chance, but there are other indications also. Frere had advocated the omission of the Decalogue and the prayer for the King. He was anxious, too, to see provision made for additional collects, epistles, and gospels.[7] Both these things were done in the schedule of 1911.

If it is true that Frere's book influenced the bishops' schedule, this may help to explain the later and quite undeniable influence which he exerted upon the alternative eucharistic rite of 1919, the first recorded instance of his advice being sought by the bishops. On that occasion Frere's influence was so overwhelming as to be inexplicable unless one may assume some such prior contact as has been suggested here.

Indeed, it is not hard to see why the sort of revision for which Frere pleaded in *Some Principles of Liturgical Reform* should have commended itself to the South African bishops as they brought out their first tentative schedule. Frere was already, by 1911, a liturgiologist of distinction, and he was deeply interested in the practical matters of Prayer Book revision. 1911 was the year in which he was appointed to the Advisory Committee on Liturgical Questions.[8] He was just the person to suit the governors of a Church which had been through the crises which had accompanied the birth of the Church of the Province. Not only was Frere a member of an official English body working on revision; his very arguments are those to which the bishops might be expected to give a favourable hearing. It is a fairly general opinion that the South African bishops were originally reluctant to move at all in

---

[7] Frere, pp. 195 ff.
[8] Jasper, *Walter Howard Frere*, p. 26.

revision. Frere begins *Some Principles of Liturgical Reform* by stressing the conservatism of the average worshipper and the need to move very slowly in making changes. This is just what we might expect the bishops to be glad to hear. Frere wrote:

In many parts of the world where the English Prayer Book is used, local and independent schemes of revision are already being undertaken. In some of these places it is, no doubt, desirable that the local scheme should come to maturity, because the local needs are sufficiently unlike our home needs to require a substantially different provision. In other parts, on the contrary, the undertaking is far less necessary; but is only the result of a natural impatience with the present unchangeableness of the Prayer Book. As regards many such areas a revised Prayer Book that would be suitable for England would be equally suitable there also; and where the work had been done at home, there would be no need for such places to prosecute an independent revision.[9]

This is intended by Frere as an argument for 'unhalting revision' in England (a revision which need not be any the less conservative for being unhalting), but might equally well be taken to be an argument for halting revision elsewhere.

Frere's approach, besides being so massively conservative, was also founded upon an acceptance of the Book of Common Prayer as a fundamentally sound and perfectly catholic book, expressive of distinctively Anglican ideas in terms of worship. He will concede that the eucharistic rite of 1662 is, in many matters of detail, unsatisfactory and in need of revision. Indeed its revision was the chief concern of his book. But he does not regard the 1662 rite (and that is to say the 1552 rite also) as being in any way a 'new' rite. It is simply the old Western rite dislocated and rearranged. It now possesses, in addition, valuable English characteristics which must not be lost. The damage must be repaired slowly and conservatively, using 1662 as the basis for all revision and beginning with a restoration of those parts of the rite which were dislocated in 1552. This is the real substance of Frere's proposals, and obviously it would accord well with the approach of South African bishops.

No doubt the bishops would have agreed with the reasons Frere advanced for desiring revision. Like Frere, they would have desired the cautious advance, for they had to consider the relations between the Church in this country on the one hand, and on the

[9] Frere, *Some Principles of Liturgical Reform*, p. 10 (cf. pp. 1, 7).

other the Church in England, the schismatics, and those in South Africa who felt that the link with England must not be further weakened. These were, of course, cogent reasons for hesitancy and it is not surprising to find the bishops following the kind of approach Frere had pleaded for, an approach which minimized the revolutionary aspect of revision by representing the new book as no more than a rearrangement of the book of 1662.

Frere had suggested that his proposed revisions need not, at first, be printed in a new or alternative Prayer Book, but might simply be added as a codicil, a list of permitted modifications.[10] Later, commenting on similar liturgical reconstruction elsewhere, Frere wrote:

The progress in Scotland has gone a good deal further than [in England]. In the appendix of the 'Code of Canons' published last year the twenty-ninth section contains 'Permissible additions to and deviations from the Service books of this Church'. The policy, that is to say, has already been adopted which many have advocated for the present stage in England, namely that changes should not be made in the text of the book, but authority should be given in certain respects to vary from the book by addition or alteration on clearly indicated lines.[11]

This kind of revision by codicil would, of course, have had the effect of further minimizing the shock, and the bishops' schedule of 1911 was, in effect, just such a codicil. It does not, however, venture even as far as the very modest proposals made by Frere. According to the minutes of episcopal synod the liturgical committee made certain recommendations in 1911 which were not included in the schedule. It is not clear from the minutes what these further suggestions were. They may have affected the eucharistic rite; but since the report of the committee is no longer extant it is impossible to tell. In adopting the provisions of the schedule of 1911 the bishops also resolved that these should not be regarded as fully and finally authoritative until they had been approved by provincial synod and until the archbishop had consulted with legal advisers on the powers of episcopal synod to make alterations to the Book of Common Prayer. The history of the Church of the Province had given cause for an almost majestic conservatism, and an unwholesome dread of the Law. The resultant schedule was a very small step forward, which did little more than collect and codify things which the bishops had

[10] Frere, p. 195.
[11] *C.Q.R.*, October 1912, p. 142.

already allowed and things which were, no doubt, already if illegally, being done. It is within the recollection of certain older priests of the Province, for instance, that as early as 1880 both the prayers after the communion were being used together at the same service.

The schedule was only a first step; but a first step implies that others are to follow. It is not easy to determine precisely how far the schedule of 1911 was intended to be a final, and how far a temporary, measure. The indications favour the supposition of a temporary measure. The bishops had already by this time appointed a committee of themselves to control all 'Prayer Book Revision and Adaptation'. This committee, variously styled 'for Prayer Book Adaptation and Enrichment', 'Prayer Book Revision', &c., but generally known as the 'Liturgical Committee', was apparently first appointed by synod on 21 November 1908 and reappointed annually thereafter. But even before that, as early as the first session of provincial synod in 1870, it had been resolved that

the bishops be requested to appoint a commission who shall prepare such services as may be further required, especially a Harvest Thanksgiving Service, which services, when they shall have obtained the unanimous approval of the Bishops of the Province, shall be enjoined for use provisionally by the authority of their Lordships.[12]

It must have been envisaged by the bishops when they eventually appointed this committee that it would have some sort of permanence. The establishment of a regular machinery for revision implies this, even if, at first, nothing more was planned than a Harvest Festival service. In fact, not long after the bishops issued their schedule of 1911, the committee prepared some revised Occasional Offices, the first really new services to be framed in South Africa.

In 1911, then, the position was that, although the bishops had left the door open for possible further revision, and although they had adopted some of the proposals contained in Frere's book, they had done nothing to suggest that they were planning a revision of the central part of the liturgy or that they were considering the adoption of even Frere's modest scheme for 'reconstituting' the English canon. Yet it was just this part of the liturgy, and of the Prayer Book as a whole, which most dissatisfied those who sought

[12] *Constitution and Canons* (1870), p. 45.

for revision at all. Even in our own day, most of the interpolating
which is done by those who find the 1662 eucharistic rite not
quite to their taste is done in those parts of the service which
surround the consecration prayer. Almost every proposal for a
revision of the 1662 rite, official or unofficial, South African or
otherwise, has contained suggestions for making considerable
changes in that prayer.

In 1913 a move was made to secure the revision of this part of
the 1662 rite. It was an unofficial proposal emanating from two
junior priests in the diocese of Grahamstown. In 1911, the same
year that the bishops issued their first tentative schedule of
modifications, the Rev. Charles Gould was appointed assistant
curate at the cathedral in Grahamstown. The relevant entry in
Crockford for 1948 (shortly before Gould died) tells us that he
had been an undergraduate at Fitzwilliam House, Cambridge, and
was ordained deacon in 1909 and priest the year after, in the
diocese of Bristol. What it does not tell us is that he had been a
Congregational minister before his ordination in the Anglican
Church, and that he was, even then, keenly interested in liturgical
matters. The fact that Gould was a liturgist before he became an
Anglican means that he was likely to have a fresher approach to
liturgical revision than most Anglicans, and was less likely to be
tied to the Book of Common Prayer by sentiment and tradition.
He had been assistant curate at St. Mary, Redcliffe, Bristol, before
coming to Grahamstown, and was subsequently to be rector of
Cathcart, of St. Paul, Port Elizabeth, rural dean of Cathcart, and
eventually a canon of Grahamstown cathedral. He joined the
army as a chaplain during the first world war, returning to the
diocese on demobilization. He later moved to the diocese of
Bloemfontein and was there rector of Kroonstad and a canon of
the cathedral.

Gould appears to have been a diligent student and a careful
reader of books, for there were among his papers after he died
several letters written to authors of liturgical studies, pointing out
errors they had made. His articles and letters, some of which will
be quoted below, make it apparent that he had a caustic wit which
made him a formidable opponent. Gould was more than a mere
dabbler in liturgiology. His knowledge was extensive, though he
never wrote any major work for publication. In 1911 the Alcuin
Club commissioned him to write a tract on Ottery St. Mary

Church, but Gould left for South Africa and the proposed book was never published. Several letters from Dr. Dearmer, the Secretary of the Alcuin Club, to Gould are now in the library of St. Paul's College in Grahamstown, and one of them presupposes considerable previous correspondence.

Two years after Gould's arrival in Grahamstown, another young priest, Jasper Bazeley, came to be subwarden of St. Paul's Hostel (now St. Paul's College) in the same city. Bazeley appears to have been of a very different character, shy, retiring, but charming, persuasive, and adventurous, and something of a mystic. The College records give us the following information about his official career. He had been at Pembroke, Oxford, and at Wells Theological College. An M.A. of Oxford and a B.D. of London, he was priested in the diocese of Norwich in 1908 and, after being assistant curate at St. Margaret, King's Lynn, was vice-principal of Sarum Theological College. From there he came to be subwarden of St. Paul's in 1913 and so remained till he became warden. In 1925 ill health, an infection of the bones of one leg, forced him to return to England. He subsequently became chaplain, first to Queen Margaret's School, Scarborough, and then to the Community of St. Denys, Warminster. He was rector of Bishopstow, Warminster, from 1930 until his death in 1934. Bazeley, too, was a student of liturgiology. He had before coming to South Africa written a lengthy essay entitled 'The Simplicity of Divine Service in the Church of England compared with the example of the Church during the First Five Centuries'. The manuscript of this essay is preserved in St. Paul's College library. Mrs. Bazeley recollects that her husband had 'won an important prize' with this essay just before he left England in 1913, the year in which he took his B.D. at London, but the records of that university contain nothing which helps to explain either the origins of the essay or the nature of the prize. There are, however, two letters from Gould to Mrs. Bazeley, written after Bazeley's death, which suggest a possible solution. Gould wrote on 23 July 1940 asking for biographical material to be included in a short history of the South African revision which he was then proposing to write. In the course of the letter he asks for 'the precise name and date of the liturgical prize which he won at Pembroke (that financed the printing of the "Revision of the Anaphora")'. In a further letter to Mrs. Bazeley, dated 23 September 1942, he said,

'One detail I need is whether the Bp. Jeune prize was awarded by Pembroke or by the University.' Whatever the origins of the essay may have been, it is clear that in it Bazeley had already begun to develop some of the ideas which later went to make up the argument of the pamphlet he later wrote with Gould, entitled *Proposals for the Revision of the Anaphora.*

In his early prize essay, 'The Simplicity of Divine Service . . .', which consists of about fifty pages of typescript, Bazeley argued that one ought not to assume:

(1) that the primitive services were simple, unless one agrees to mean by that term any form which is assumed spontaneously and at an early stage of development;

(2) that the early forms of service represented fully the ideals of the leaders and saints of the time; or

(3) that what seemed best for them is necessarily best for us.

The essay consists, first of all, of a comparison of the liturgy of St. James and other primitive rites with that of 1662; and, secondly, of an examination of the origins of the 1662 Choir Offices. In the essay Bazeley used for his type of the primitive liturgy a conflation and compression, contrived by himself, of the liturgies of St. James (in both the Greek and the Syriac versions), St. Basil, St. Mark, and St. John Chrysostom, and also (as secondary sources) the *Apostolic Constitutions,* the Prayer Book of Sarapion, the *Catechetical Lectures* of St. Cyril, the writings of St. John Chrysostom, and *De Sacramentis.* His conclusions are not at all what the title of the essay seems at first sight to suggest, for he tends to regard the 'simplicity' of 1662 as an unnecessary impoverishment of the rite. Bazeley, then, had no more reason than Gould to be particularly sympathetic or tender towards the form of the liturgy found in 1662 and hitherto preserved inviolate by the bishops of the Province. Bazeley found the simplicity of the Prayer Book a fault; Gould had become a liturgiologist before he was an Anglican. But both were agreed that an extensive revision of the book was desirable. Both were, quite evidently, acquainted with a good deal of liturgical scholarship and were at least adequately equipped to frame a proposed form of revision to serve as a basis of discussion.

This they proceeded to do. Since Gould left the cathedral in Grahamstown in 1914 and Bazeley had only arrived at St. Paul's in 1913, they were not together for any great length of time; but within a few months of Bazeley's arrival they began work upon an interesting liturgical experiment later embodied in pamphlet form in the *Proposals*. Their chief desire was to substitute for the consecration prayer of 1662 an anaphora composed upon more primitive and catholic lines.

They read a paper to a group of clergymen in Grahamstown, giving the reasons for the changes they proposed, and the paper, enthusiastically received by those who heard it read, was privately printed in 1913. Only a few copies of it now exist, though there are several in St. Paul's College library. The original group of clergymen consisted of the dean and the chancellor of the cathedral and one of the canons. The chancellor was the Rev. E. C. West, Bazeley's warden at St. Paul's. The other member of the 'Grahamstown group' was the Rev. F. R. Phelps, at that time chaplain to the Community of the Resurrection in Grahamstown, and later first dean and then bishop of Grahamstown, and eventually archbishop of Cape Town.

The group sent a copy of the paper and of the proposed anaphora to the bishop, Dr. Cornish, the then chairman of the committee on Prayer Book Revision and Adaptation (Liturgical Committee), requesting him to forward the proposals to his committee and to allow copies to be sent to all the clergy of the diocese. This the bishop agreed to do, though no direct mention of *Proposals* in the records of either the episcopal synod or of the liturgical committee can now be found. Bishop Cornish himself went on to advise that copies of the paper 'should be sent to those in England . . . engaged in the same work'.[13] The bishop agreed to allow copies to be sent to the clergy of the diocese, and indeed it appears that after the pamphlet had been printed, it was circulated not only in the diocese of Grahamstown but also in the Province at large and among sympathizers in England. In the pamphlet there appeared: a short preface, the correspondence which had passed between Bishop Cornish and the 'Grahamstown group', the original paper (chiefly Bazeley's work), the proposed anaphora (the joint work of Bazeley and Gould), and three appendices contributed by Gould after the paper had been read to the group. Gould's appendices were chiefly concerned with the invocation used in the proposed anaphora.

The anaphora, revolutionary and unofficial, was the main concern of *Proposals*. The authors did not make any suggestions

[13] *Proposals*, p. v.

as to the rest of the rite though they did propose a rearrangement
of the order of certain prayers. The pamphlet was simply what
it claimed to be, a proposal for a radical reconstruction of the
consecration prayer. It used the 1662 prayer for one part of the
new anaphora, but for the rest it drew upon quite other sources.
Such a scheme struck right at the heart of the official plan for
revision adopted by the bishops of the Province, and it called for
something which could not be disguised as a merely permissive
and unimportant alternative to the Book of Common Prayer.
Nor was it a reorganization of liturgical factors gleaned from
English Prayer Books, such as Frere had advocated. *Proposals* was
an attempt to displace the central and most sacrosanct part of 1662
by a new anaphora, constructed on a quite new pattern, and it
would have made of 1662 an unmistakably new and different rite.

Other young clergymen have dreamed of revolutionary
measures and nothing much has come of them, but Bazeley and
Gould had secured the interest of the senior dignitaries of the
diocese. We do not know what the bishops' reaction was when
Proposals was brought to their notice, but the reaction of others
in the country is recorded. The magazine of the diocese of Pretoria
contained in February 1914 the following report:

In 1913[14] the bishops of the Province issued a list of suggestions and
adaptations of the services, which was welcomed, because as revision
was in the air, it seemed good and right to make provisional experiments before the work of revision was done; partly because a living
church must grow, and have elasticity to adapt itself to the varying
needs of every age.

After this surely exaggerated description of the bishops' work, the
article continued:

A small pamphlet written by Mr. Bazeley and Mr. Gould . . . goes
beyond any suggestions that were made by the bishops for it suggests
the complete revision of the anaphora.

There follows a fair and reasonable summary of the main points
of *Proposals*, and the article ends:

But most people would very much like to see the Liturgy rearranged
with some additions and improvements, while all are conservative
enough to want to keep the old words and phrases they have been used
to, and that generations of their forefathers have used. So a revised

---

[14] This must be an error for 1911. A schedule agreed on by episcopal synod in
1911 would probably not have been published and issued until 1912.

Liturgy is certain not to please everyone, and until parishes are used to it, it is probable that it will please no one, in spite of the general wish for improvement.[15]

This article probably did not entirely reflect the official policy of the bishops, but it does represent the sort of attitude of mind for which the bishops had been catering. Official policy thus far had been to use 1662 as the norm and basis for the liturgy, and gradually by means of a schedule of permissible deviations, rather than by framing an alternative rite, to shape it into something more nearly approaching what was then desired. The great disadvantage of this method, in that it had the effect of creating not two alternative rites but as many different rites as there were possible combinations of the schedule and the original rite, seems to have escaped notice. The schedule was, however, only a temporary expedient. The chaos which might have resulted if this policy had been pursued had mercifully never to be faced.

By retaining 1662 as the basic and only official rite, the bishops might hope to pacify those who preferred, for whatever reason, the Book of Common Prayer as it stood. They had taken as their guide one intimately connected with revision in England and they might have argued that they were doing no more than was being done in England, for in England at the time the situation was very similar. In 1914 the Lower House of Convocation had voted for a permissible rearrangement of the 1662 liturgy, somewhat along the lines advocated by Frere. The Upper House had, however, vetoed the proposal.[16]

The South African bishops did not allow themselves, then, to be much affected by the *Proposals*, whatever their opinion of the merits and demerits of the work may have been. Episcopal synod did, however, issue a new schedule of permitted modifications in 1915,[17] but these did not in any way affect the liturgy. For the most part the schedule of 1915 was simply the schedule of 1911 reissued, but now also authorized by provincial synod. The schedule of 1911 had carried a note to the effect that the adaptations were

[15] *Historical Records*, pp. 227 f. The article is not reprinted in *Historical Records* exactly as it first appeared in *The Kingdom* (magazine of the diocese of Pretoria), XI, no. 2, February 1914, p. 7. It has been adapted and shortened and no acknowledgement is made of the fact that this has been done.

[16] Jasper, *Walter Howard Frere*, pp. 56 ff.

[17] *Prayers upon Several Occasions and Modifications of Services* (Church of the Province of South Africa, 1915).

put forth by the Bishop of the Diocese for the use of the clergy and laity. They will, if it be found desirable, be submitted to the next Provincial Synod. In the meantime they are put forth provisionally, in view of the advice of the last Lambeth Conference, with a view to ascertaining whether they meet certain expressed needs.

The 1915 schedule was the result of this experiment. Its provisions, where they affected the eucharistic rite, marked no change from 1911. The bishops seem to have assumed that each parish would have at least one celebration of the eucharist each Sunday. The provincial synod had resolved in 1870 that it was desirable that the holy communion should be celebrated every Sunday and feast day at an early hour. It is impossible to tell how soon this became an almost universal custom, but it is highly probable that it had happened by the beginning of this century. Even after the 1915 schedule had been published, this early celebration would have had to be the service of 1662 in its entirety, except for the omission of the Longer Exhortation and the use of both the 1662 post-communion prayers. If a second service came later in the day, as was very probable under South African conditions (particularly in the country districts where each parish included several villages and hamlets), it might vary somewhat from the norm. The rite might pick up from the *Kyries* at the end of the litany and proceed from there (after the prayer of St. Chrysostom) to the Collect, Epistle, and Gospel. After that, the service would again be 1662 in its entirety. Thus, after fifty-five years of hesitant revision, the anaphora itself remained that of 1662, unaltered and unadorned.

CHAPTER TWO

A REVOLUTIONARY
CONSECRATION PRAYER

Proposals for the Revision of the Anaphora called for a thorough-going reversal of the previous and official policy. Gould asserted many years later in a chapter contributed to *Historical Records*[1] that he and Bazeley had been much influenced by the work of W. C. Bishop. The chief medium for this influence seems to have been an article which Bishop had published in the *Church Quarterly Review* for July 1908. This article is entitled 'The Primitive Form of Consecration' and is several times either quoted or referred to in the *Proposals*. Another article of Bishop's, 'The Mass in Spain', from the *Church Quarterly Review* for January 1907, was also used by Bazeley and Gould. According to a biographical note introducing a volume of essays and articles written by Bishop and published after his death by the Alcuin Club under the title *The Mozarabic and Ambrosian Rites*, all of his writing took the form of articles contributed to the *Church Quarterly Review*, and they are, therefore, apart from the few reprinted in that collection, now no longer easily accessible.

But W. C. Bishop was an able liturgiologist of considerable reputation. He is, for instance, the only Anglican scholar whose theories Dr. Adrian Fortescue thought worth taking into consideration in his book on the Roman mass.[2] The fairly long and detailed summary of Bishop's hypothesis which Fortescue gives is based upon the very article of which Bazeley and Gould made so much use, and is now probably the source of most people's knowledge of Bishop's views. Fortescue, however, uses only such parts of the article as bear directly upon the Roman rite. Some of Bishop's arguments are to be found repeated in part in *The Mozarabic and Ambrosian Rites*. But even these sources do not by any means cover the whole argument put forward by Bishop and, in view of the importance of Bishop's influence upon the *Proposals*,

---

[1] pp. 288 ff. *N.B.* p. 292.
[2] A. Fortescue, *The Mass* (2 ed., Longmans, 1914), pp. 146 ff.

it is desirable to have the substance of his hypothesis clearly summarized.

The purpose of 'The Primitive Form of Consecration'[3] is a reconstruction of the earliest type of anaphora used by the Church. Bishop is concerned more with the 'form' or pattern of the anaphora than with the theology of consecration; so he pleads that the historical problem, the reconstruction of the form or pattern, should be approached without any doctrinal presuppositions. His introductory remarks are designed to show that the supposed difference in this respect between East and West has been exaggerated. The general conclusions to which he comes are these:

(1) that at an early date all liturgies followed the present Eastern *pattern* of Institution, Anamnesis, and Invocation; and that the West at a later date departed from that pattern.

(2) that at the very least one cannot be certain that the Roman canon has not been altered from some such supposed original.

(3) that there is no reason to doubt the primitive *order of the parts* of the Eastern anaphora, and none for depending on the Roman.

(4) that *Supplices te* cannot (because of its elaborate language) be considered an earlier form of the Invocation than its Eastern counterpart; nor can one suppose that in the primitive rites the Invocation ever preceded the words of Institution.[4]

Although the Deir Balizeh fragments had been discovered by the time that Bishop wrote this article (1908), their contents do not seem to have become widely known at that date. The fragments do not seem to have been edited and published until 1909.[5]

The historical inquiry by which Bishop arrived at these conclusions is a lengthy one, covering each of the main families of liturgies in turn, and indicating how each of them is constructed upon a pattern which is generally constant. The article is really a claim that the primitive consecration prayer was a general thanksgiving for all God's saving mercies to man, arranged in a logical (that is to say, historical) order. To this thanksgiving, he argues, there was added at the most suitable points those three things which specifically relate it to the Last Supper—the narrative of the institution, the offering to God of the elements of the rite,

---

[3] *C.Q.R.*, LXVI, pp. 385 ff.
[4] pp. 403 f. The italics are mine.
[5] Cf. Salaville, *Eastern Liturgies* (English translation, Sands, 1938), p. 20, and Srawley, *The Early History of the Liturgy* (2 ed., Cambridge University Press, 1947), p. 58 n.

and the invocation which sums up the purpose of the whole prayer. This provides, as it were, a secondary logical order superimposed upon the thanksgivings. This double order is, in Bishop's view, the primitive pattern of the anaphora.

The earliest definite traditional pattern we possess is that of the Eastern liturgies, and this form probably represents, with only unimportant changes in the wording not in the meaning, the oecumenical tradition of the early ages.[6]

Such a reconstruction of the primitive pattern would probably be at least partly accepted by a good many modern scholars. Dix has put forward the tentative suggestion that the 'thanksgivings' may well prove to be the most primitive part of the anaphora, and the basis of such uniformity as there was in the practice of the primitive Church.[7] Cirlot agrees generally with Bishop's supposition that the words of institution, the oblation and the invocation have been fitted into the pattern of thanksgivings.[8]

Lietzmann's hypothesis that there were two quite distinct original forms of the eucharist would, if proved, destroy the force of Bishop's appeal to the universal character of his pattern. But Lietzmann's theory confronts one with a considerable problem in that the documentary sources upon which he has based his argument are all subject to a wide variety of interpretation. No one, for instance, has yet been able to fix exactly either the date or the place of origin of the *Didaché*. Even those who champion the authoritative conservatism of the *Apostolic Tradition* of Hippolytus admit that the history of its author raises serious questions about the contents of his treatise. Sarapion's rite, again, may have been no more than a primitive and local variation of the early Alexandrian rite. The eighth book of the *Apostolic Constitutions* is viewed in so many different lights that it is difficult to speak about it at all without getting upon debated ground. Not one of these documents can safely be called an authoritative liturgy in use at some definite place at some fixed time. Upon these, and upon his interpretation of them, Lietzmann's argument depends. It may be held that there are no more authoritative sources than these. However true this may be, until such time as more cogent proof can be advanced to show that Lietzmann's documents are

[6] *C.Q.R.*, LXVI, p. 404.
[7] G. Dix, *The Shape of the Liturgy* (2 ed., Dacre Press: A. & C. Black, 1945), pp. 217 ff.
[8] *The Early Eucharist* (S.P.C.K., 1939), pp. 51, 61 ff., 69 f.

authoritative enough to bear the weight of argument which he places upon them, his view must be regarded as hypothetical.

Even *ex hypothesi*, Lietzmann is not really destructive of Bishop's theory. If the early eucharist did not contain the thanksgivings,[9] then it is extremely difficult to explain how such a peculiarly Jewish feature should have been introduced into the liturgy in a predominantly Gentile church. All the rites Lietzmann uses contain a thanksgiving. Even the Egyptian rite is no exception. In any event, the evidence Lietzmann cites as touching this rite is patient of a different interpretation from that which he employs. Sarapion's rite may well be regarded as evidence for the fact that in Egypt the *Sanctus*, institution, anamnesis, and invocation were introduced into the Great Thanksgiving *at different points* from those of the Eastern rites; a supposition which would support Bishop's contention that the thanksgivings are the oldest part of the prayer. Finally, Lietzmann admits that the Thanksgiving was typical of his primitive 'Pauline' rite—and it is from this rite that, in his view, almost all the later liturgies evolved.[10] Even—if Lietzmann is right—in the Jerusalem type, the blessing of the bread was by thanksgiving.

Positive support for Bishop's hypothesis is to be found in E. G. P. Wyatt's *The Eucharistic Prayer*, a great deal of which is devoted to an attempt to demonstrate that the Roman canon once followed the pattern now found in most Eastern anaphoras.[11]

It was Bishop's reconstruction of a supposedly universal pattern for the anaphora which chiefly attracted Bazeley and Gould. The argument of *Proposals* is principally devoted to supporting Bishop's hypothesis. It begins with an examination of the earliest liturgies. The evidence cited by the authors is in no way remarkable; it consists chiefly of phrases in I *Clement* 59, 60, which are echoed in *A.C. VIII*, the 'technical' use of the term *Eucharist* in Ignatius, *Ep. ad Smyrn.* 8, and the usual references to Justin Martyr, I *Apology* xiii 65, 67. It becomes clear thus early in the pamphlet that the authors' main purpose is to stress the element of thanksgiving in the early anaphoras. But Bazeley and Gould do not always follow W. C. Bishop so closely in matters of detail. They leave aside the bulk of the early evidence he cited, and turn instead

[9] Lietzmann, *Mass and Lord's Supper* (English translation, E. J. Brill, Leiden, 1954), p. 136.
[10] Lietzmann, pp. 186 f. (cf. pp. 209 ff.).
[11] E. G. P. Wyatt, *The Eucharistic Prayer* (Alcuin Club, 1914), pp. 21 ff.

to the third century. They quote the *Canons of Hippolytus*[12] for the *Sursum corda* and words of administration. They cite Cyprian, *On the Lord's Prayer*, 20, as quoting the *Sursum corda*, and Clement's use of the *Sanctus* in conjunction with Daniel vii. 10. Neither reference is entirely clear, but it is obviously the intention of the authors to maintain that the *Sursum corda* and *Sanctus* are of early origin.[13] Bishop's point of view was rather different.

When Bazeley and Gould turn to consider later liturgies, their dependence upon Bishop is, again, not marked. They prefer Duchesne's classification of the families of rites[14] to Bishop's— though they reject with scorn Duchesne's hypothesis that the Alexandrian liturgy was derived from the Roman. At this point and without any further preliminaries, the authors of *Proposals* seize upon the liturgy of the *Apostolic Constitutions* (*A.C. VIII*) as the ideal type of the primitive liturgy. They hasten to add that they do not believe that this liturgy was ever used. They argue, instead, that the man who compiled *A.C. VIII* must have been familiar with a very similar rite. In view of the startling differences between Bazeley and Gould's own compilation and the rite with which they were most familiar (1662), we may be allowed to regard this assumption with reserve. Bazeley and Gould do not make it clear why they prefer *A.C. VIII* to any other early liturgy, but simply inform the reader that the anaphora of *A.C. VIII* is to be regarded as the best model of primitive rites, and proceed to a long and detailed analysis of the commemorations contained in it.

Gould added three appendices to *Proposals*. In the first of these he argued, on the basis of I *Clement* 24 and the liturgies of St. James and of St. Cyril's lectures, that the *Sanctus* aspires to link the eucharist with the worship of heaven. He composed an alternative Preface which brings out this idea very clearly. This may explain why Bazeley and Gould attempted to show that the *Sanctus* was an early feature of the anaphora and include one in their own proposed prayer, in spite of the fact that they quote Bishop's view that it was not an original and primitive part of the form. Bishop had argued that the *Sanctus* in *A.C. VIII* was of later provenance

---

[12] From Duchesne, *Christian Worship* (3rd English ed.), pp. 525 ff.; cf. 5th English ed. (S.P.C.K., 1931), pp. 529 ff.

[13] Cyprian, *de Orat. Dom.* cxxxi, has a reference to the *Sursum corda*. The reference to Clement must be I *Clement* 34.

[14] Duchesne, p. 55 (cf. Bishop in *C.Q.R.*, LXVI, pp. 387 f.).

than the thanksgivings.[15] Bazeley and Gould retain it, though when they come to the *Benedictus qui venit*, they hold that this is a late feature and omit it altogether from their anaphora.

After the authors of the pamphlet have expressed their preference for *A.C. VIII* as the best type to be followed, they proceed to a comparison of this rite with the liturgies of St. James, St. Basil, and St. Chrysostom, and note the points at which each of these differs from the norm of *A.C. VIII*. It is worth noting that the third of Gould's appendices is an abbreviated translation of the common features of the Greek and Syriac versions of St. James. This condensed anaphora is not identical with the version Bishop included in his article discussed above; nor with that 'reconstructed' by Bazeley in 'The Simplicity of Divine Service . . .'. No doubt Gould provided this adaptation of St. James as an additional foundation for the argument of the pamphlet in case *A.C. VIII* should not seem as convincingly authoritative to the reader as it was to the authors.

The argument which *Proposals* presents thus far is best summed up as an attempt to show that in the early ages the celebrant's train of thought was expected to follow a series of commemorations, giving thanks for God's revelation of himself to man over the whole scheme of history from creation to Pentecost. Normally the authors hold, supplication is only introduced into this scheme at the memorial of Pentecost where the mention of the Holy Spirit provides a natural link with the invocation. This feature, they would have us believe, is the climax of the anaphora as early as the time of the Council of Nicea. The latter part of the pamphlet is a particular and detailed examination of the nature of the primitive invocation. It adds nothing to the argument and the evidence cited is in no way out of the ordinary. The conclusion to which Bazeley and Gould come is that 'some kind of invocation of the Divine assistance was universal and that there is no hint (except possibly in *De Sacramentis* iv. 23) of a theory that the recitation of the words of Institution alone would suffice'.[16]

---

[15] *C.Q.R.*, LXVI, p. 388.
[16] *Proposals*, p. 10. The evidence cited by Bazeley and Gould to establish the nature of the primitive invocation is:
Justin Martyr, 1 *Apology* i. 66.
Irenaeus, *Adv. Haer.* IV. xviii. 6.
Tertullian, *Ad Marcion.* iv. 40.
Origen as quoted by Warren in *Liturgy of the Ante-Nicene Church*, p. 121.
[*continued on next page*

Unfortunately they immediately went beyond what their evidence warranted and stated categorically that a fully developed Eastern type of invocation was a feature of the primitive anaphora. Such an invocation formed a part of the proposed prayer appended to their pamphlet. Gould, moreover, devoted the third of his appendices to an examination of the invocation of the English rite of 1549. His hypothesis is that Cranmer based the 1549 invocation upon *Quam oblationem* of the Latin canon; and taking this to be an invocation thought its position a legitimate one. Gould, therefore, rejects the possibility that 1549 might serve as a pattern for reconstructing an Anglican anaphora.

In the text of the pamphlet there is next a critique of some contemporary theories of the origin of the Roman rite. Bazeley and Gould assert that similarities between Eastern and Western anaphoras are too great to be coincidental, and must be due either to a common origin and constant interchange of ideas or to wholesale importation. This dilemma does not exhaust all the possible hypotheses, however, and it is obviously unsatisfactory. Phrases like 'common origin' require careful definition, and it is difficult to see what real distinction there is between 'constant interchange of ideas' and 'wholesale importation'. The former phrase merely has a more pleasant sound. The 'wholesale importation' hypothesis used by Duchesne to account for some of the non-Roman Western rites[17] is rejected with scorn by the authors of *Proposals*. Their alternative theory is that the Western anaphoras all originally followed the same pattern as the Eastern and were gradually made to conform to the Roman type. This does not, of course, explain the origin of the Roman pattern. All that the authors say of it is that, far from being the mother-liturgy of the

---

note 16 *continued from previous page*]

Athanasius as quoted by Stone in *Doctrine of the Holy Eucharist*, vol. I, p. 70.
Chrysostom as quoted in Brightman, *Liturgies Eastern and Western*, vol. I, pp. 474, 479.
Cyril, *Catechetical Lectures*, XIX.
Ambrose, *De Myst.* 54, and *De Fide* iv. 124.
Pseudo-Ambrose, *De Sacramentis* iv. 23.
Optatus as quoted by Gore in *Body of Christ*, p. 84.
Gelasius as quoted by Routh in *Script. Eccle. Op.*, vol. II. p. 39, and by Fortescue in *The Mass*, p. 406 n.
See *Proposals*, pp. 10 ff. (footnotes). If the material listed here were as decisive as Bazeley and Gould assumed, the controversy over primitive consecration prayers would have been settled long ago.
[17] *Christian Worship*, p. 93.

West, it was thrust upon it 'by pope and Frankish king, or on England by the ultramontanes between Whitby and Cloveshoo'.[18] There is only one primitive type and the Roman rite is an inferior deviation from it; 'inferior in rationality, method, and catholic authority. It was adopted, partly under pressure, partly in zeal for the Roman and imperial idea, and partly, if not chiefly, because the clergy were too ignorant to manage the elaborations of the old Western rites'.[19]

When Bazeley and Gould come to state the practical application of their hypothesis they appeal for a reversal of this trend by which the Roman canon became the norm for Western Christendom. The alternatives as stated in *Proposals* are either to leave 1662 unchanged and face the prospect of illegal interpolation or to adopt the Gregorian canon complete with all its faults. The one possibility not envisaged is just that kind of compromise which was reflected in the South African final form. The authors of *Proposals* claimed to have based their own attempt at reconstructing a non-Roman anaphora on two fundamental principles: to make use of every existing phrase of the 1662 consecration prayer, and to bring these phrases into harmony with the fourth-century pattern.

The fourth century is an odd choice for liturgical scholars who claim to be following W. C. Bishop, but it is in keeping with the rest of the pamphlet. Most of the patristic evidence cited is from the third and fourth centuries, and Bishop's attempt to reconstruct a *second-century* anaphora is ignored. Other points of difference between Bishop and the authors of *Proposals* have already been noted. Bishop himself commented on one of the differences in a letter to Gould dated 20 March 1914.

My Dear Sir,
    The pamphlet arrived yesterday, with your letter; and I have read through the pamphlet, but hope to do so more carefully by and by. If it had only come a few days earlier I could have reviewed it for the forthcoming no. of C.Q.R. But it's just too late to be included in an article on three other books of the same kind which I have written for this no.
    I applaud your courage in returning to the early liturgies instead of (as many do) looking only to former revisions of the Prayerbook. But

[18] *Proposals*, p. 13.
[19] *Proposals*, p. 14.

I prefer my own restoration of the 4th century[20] form of St. James (in an article The Primitive Form of Consecration) anaphora to the one which you give. The bits which I have left out are those which appear to me to have evidently been added about the 5th century—and are characterized by turgidity and an artificial piling up of epithets and clauses from which the earlier form (as I take it) was freer.

Bazeley and Gould deliberately chose the fourth century as their model because:

(i) it is the first period which has left us a complete liturgy;

(ii) it is the earliest in which the doctrines of the Church were taught in the technical terms which have become universal; and

(iii) it is the latest at which there is any high degree of uniformity in Christendom.[21]

Next the authors assert that an anaphora based on the fourth-century pattern could exclude no catholic ceremonial, since all ceremonial has been fitted into this pattern in the course of subsequent history, often without the introduction of new ritual. On the other hand the fourth-century anaphora does not positively require any ceremonial other than is necessary for the performance of any rite.

Finally, the authors justify their use of Greek rather than Latin sources:

(i) because they are truer to primitive type in their orderly arrangement.

(ii) because so doing reduces the loss in translation, for the Latin in most cases is probably based on a Greek original.

(iii) our information on the Keltic use is only sufficient to assure us that it was of the Gallican type, but it tells us little of the pre-Roman canon. If we act upon this one piece of information and turn to Gaul, we find it almost impossible to distinguish what was normal or early amidst that vast variety.

(iv) there is much to be said for turning to Jerusalem in prayer.[22]

The last of these four grounds for preferring Greek sources comes as a shock to the reader. The metaphor is quaint to the point of obscurity. To Bazeley and Gould 'turning to Jerusalem' meant making use of the ancient liturgy of Jerusalem, but they do not

---

[20] Although in this letter Bishop refers to his own '4th century form of St. James', in the original article referred to it is clear that he there thought of it as the second century form of the anaphora (*C.Q.R.*, LXVI, pp. 388, 400 ff.).

[21] *Proposals*, p. 14.

[22] *Proposals*, p. 15.

specifically say so. There has been nothing in *Proposals* to prepare for a turning to Jerusalem even in the metaphorical sense.

We have seen how the authors preferred *A.C. VIII* to St. James. We have seen how they followed W. C. Bishop in general and yet did not make use of his reconstruction of a second-century St. James. Then, without warning, there is this leap from imaginative to serious thinking. For a moment it seems that the authors are going to follow Bishop in his preference for an early form of St. James after all, especially when it is noted that Gould devotes the second of his appendices to a translation of that rite. 'In the main,' so the argument of the *Proposals* runs, 'it [St. James] agrees marvellously with St. Cyril's lectures and with the liturgy of the *Apostolic Constitutions*. Anyhow it is the nearest we can get to antiquity . . .'; but immediately after this, and there seems to be a *non sequitur* in the argument, they go on to say, '. . . so, having decided to follow the liturgy of the *Apostolic Constitutions* in outline, except where it wanders from the logical sequence and from all other liturgies, the compilers have picked their phrases where they could get good authority and a not too un-English idea'.[23] *A.C. VIII* is preferred to St. James after all. Perhaps the explanation of this apparent uncertainty is to be found in the fact that the pamphlet was the work of two men in collaboration. Perhaps Gould preferred St. James, as his second appendix might seem to show, while Bazeley preferred *A.C. VIII*. But in his essay, 'The Simplicity of Divine Service', Bazeley had used St. James as his primary source, and *A.C. VIII* only as secondary to it. In *Proposals* the position is reversed. Even though it is difficult to explain this muddle, it is very clear that St. James and *A.C. VIII* are the two chief sources for the anaphora attached to *Proposals*. The authors have also made use of phrases from the 1549, 1662, and Scottish rites. It would seem that Bazeley and Gould had also consulted the Non-Jurors' liturgy, for they assert that they have themselves arrived at approximately the same result, though by an independent route. The reference given for the Non-Jurors' liturgy is Darwell Stone's *Doctrine of the Holy Eucharist*, vol. II (pages 480 ff.). The text of the Non-Jurors' anaphora of 1718 given by Stone does agree fairly well in content and order with the anaphora of *Proposals*. In both, for instance, the *Amen* is retained after the words of institution, giving an immediate

[23] *Proposals*, p. 15.

appearance of similarity. But the Non-Jurors used hardly anything from 1662 and they did not include any variable propers within the consecration prayer itself. The first part of the Non-Jurors' anaphora is longer and more diffuse, and the oblation and invocation shorter, than the corresponding parts of Bazeley and Gould's rite.

The authors conveniently printed a list of sources used in compiling their anaphora, and this, with a system of marginal references used by them, makes it possible to analyse the prayer exactly into its component parts. The sources used were *A.C. VIII*, St. Basil, St. Chrysostom, St. Mark, St. James and the Nestorian liturgy from Brightman's *Liturgies Eastern and Western*, Neale's essay on the Gallican rite in *Essays in Liturgiology*, the *Catechetical Lectures* of St. Cyril, and the Mozarabic mass used to illustrate W. C. Bishop's article 'The Mass in Spain' (reprinted in *The Mozarabic and Ambrosian Rites*).

From this congeries of source material Bazeley and Gould constructed their proposed anaphora. They directed that it was to follow the Comfortable Words in the 1662 rite. After the *Sursum corda* the anaphora follows the 1662 words as far as the end of the preface, when there is a thanksgiving for creation. At Trinity the 1662 proper preface for that feast takes the place of this thanksgiving, as does the Scottish preface for saints on most Red Letter days. A thanksgiving for the angels and the *Sanctus* follows and then there is a commemoration of the Law and the Prophets, which is invariable, and of the Incarnation, which varies at Christmas, Epiphany, and on feasts of Our Lady. The 1662 consecration prayer serves as a fixed commemoration of the passion and institution. The anamnesis follows, based chiefly upon that of the Scottish rite, and varies at Easter, Ascension, and Whitsun, when it is replaced by the 1662 preface proper to those seasons. The invocation is invariable and is introduced by the words 'Hear us, O merciful Father . . .' from 1662. The 1662 prayer of Oblation follows, with very little change, and is followed in turn by the Lord's prayer and the prayer of Humble Access. The 1662 words of administration are replaced by an invitation based on the 1552 form of the words and a form of administration which is, in fact, the form of 1549 without 'which was given/shed for thee'. If a second consecration is required, the priest is directed to consecrate again *in both kinds*, using the whole prayer from 'Our Saviour

Christ' to 'all other benefits of his passion'. This admirably consistent direction is important in view of the controversy which was
later to centre round the question of a second consecration.

The framework of the 1662 rite as a whole remained intact.
The parts of the service in which the congregation join, and the
words introducing these parts, are unchanged. The whole of the
1662 prayers of Consecration and Oblation are incorporated into
the new anaphora, and a place is found for each of the proper
prefaces. The new material in the prayer makes up about half of
its total length. Of this, half again is based upon the language of
either *A.C. VIII* or St. James. These are, as might be expected,
by far the most important of the sources. The Scottish rite, that is
to say the Communion Office of 1912 of the Episcopal Church in
Scotland, contributes one of the propers and two or three other
short passages. St. Mark, St. Basil, and St. Chrysostom provide
most of the rest, and a few phrases are drawn from St. Cyril's
lectures and from the Nestorian liturgy. Two clauses are added
direct from the Roman mass, but there is no verbal dependence
upon any non-Roman Western source.

Some of the additions have, for us, an unfamiliar sound, and
some have that lifelessness which one has come to expect of translations of long-disused liturgies. In the *post-sanctus*, for instance,
there is the clause 'For thou indeed art most high and most holy,
and we bless thee and we thank thee . . .'; and in the proper for
Saints' days, '. . . for all thy gifts, known to us and unknown, we
give thanks unto thee . . .'. Most of the work, however, is
extremely well done. The English used to translate phrases
drawn from ancient liturgies is for the most part already familiar
because it appears also in the Authorized Version of the Bible and
in the Book of Common Prayer. The ferial preface is a good
example of this apt use of familiar language:

O Lord, Holy Father, of whom all fatherhood in heaven and earth is
named; Almighty King, the author and giver of all good things;
everlasting God, the same yesterday, today and forever; who didst
create all things visible and invisible, through thine only begotten Son;
who givest life and grace and wisdom through thy Holy Spirit.

According to the authors' marginal references the passage is based
chiefly upon *A.C. VIII*, but the actual language is taken from the
1662 preface, Hebrews xiii, the collect for Trinity VI, and the
Nicene Creed. There is, in fact, very little of the language of the

proposed anaphora which is unsuitable, or could not easily be made suitable, for use in church.

Bishop Fisher, Bazeley's predecessor as subwarden at St. Paul's and at a later date chairman of the liturgical committee, has expressed the opinion, in private conversation, that the credit for the felicitous use of familiar and rhythmical phrases ought to be given to Gould. It is worth comparing the memorial of creation in *Proposals* with the 'typical liturgy' compiled by Bazeley in 'The Simplicity of Divine Service'. In the latter this thanksgiving runs:

Who didst make man from the earth after thine image and when he transgressed thy commandment and fell thou didst not disregard nor leave him, O good God, but didst correct him as a tender father, didst call him by the Law, and didst educate him by the prophets.

The corresponding passage in *Proposals* reads:

Who . . . having made man after thine image, didst not, when he fell, forsake him, but didst call and teach him by the Law and the Prophets.

In each the marginal references indicate that the passage is modelled on *A.C. VIII* and St. James, but the second is shorter, less verbose, and certainly more happily phrased. A good deal of Eastern prolixity has been eliminated. It may well be that the improvement is due to Gould's influence, though it is possible that it is to be explained quite simply by the fact that Bazeley composed his earlier 'typical liturgy' for the academic purpose of comparison with 1662 and was not concerned with matters of literary style.

At all events the rite of *Proposals* does for the most part escape the foreign, stilted style, so noticeable, for instance, in translations of the Roman missal intended for use in Anglican worship. Almost certainly this is owing to the fact that the proposed anaphora was a composition and not a translation. Bazeley and Gould showed themselves competent and imaginative in welding the whole of their anaphora together, and particularly in their neat use of the 1662 proper prefaces. Undoubtedly the large number of variable parts from which the celebrant would have had to select that which was appropriate to the day was a factor militating against their anaphora's adoption by the Province. Sometimes, indeed, the break comes in mid-sentence and the eye has to travel down as much as half a page to find the next clause. This inconvenience might have been overcome in practice by printing the whole anaphora proper to each feast and season in the part of the missal which contains the other propers, collects, epistles, and gospels.

This clumsiness apart, *Proposals* represents an admirable attempt to translate competent scholarship into a workable modern rite, but it had little effect upon the final form of the South African rite. In most cases where the language of *Proposals* is similar to that of the South African form, the similarity is due to a common dependence upon either 1662 or the Scottish rite. Where both have borrowed from the Scottish form, the present South African rite is nearer the original than it is to *Proposals*. It is not likely, therefore, that the borrowing is a mediate one, through *Proposals*.

The only phrase from the whole of the anaphora proposed by Bazeley and Gould which has found its way into the final South African rite is the phrase 'to take our nature upon him', used by Bazeley and Gould in the thanksgiving for the Incarnation. In the South African anaphora the phrase is joined to the 1662 words 'and suffer death upon the cross for our redemption'. It is just possible that this phrase is to be traced to the liturgy of the Lusitanian Church.[24] Gould certainly at one time possessed a copy of this liturgy but there is no way of telling at what date it came into his possession. No reference is made to it among the sources used for compiling the proposed anaphora. The Lusitanian form of the phrase is slightly different from that used in *Proposals*, and it seems more likely that Bazeley and Gould used the Christmas Collect of the Book of Common Prayer (where the wording is identical) as their source. They may have borrowed the *idea* from the Lusitanian rite, though, of course, it was also to be found in several of their avowed sources. The Rev. W. Lockton, in reviewing the South African *Proposed Form* of 1918 (in which the phrase also appeared), recognized it as being part of the Christmas Collect, though he criticized it as an insufficient memorial of the Incarnation.[25] Lockton was apparently unaware that the phrase had also appeared in *Proposals*. The use of such a phrase, drawn from some other part of 1662, to express an idea found in the ancient liturgies, is exactly what one would expect of Bazeley and Gould.

[24] Cf. Pope and Clough, *The Divine Offices of the Reformed Episcopal Churches of Spain and Portugal* (Partridge & Co., 1882), p. 106.

[25] *C.Q.R.*, LXXXVI, p. 345.

There is one other part of *Proposals*, though not strictly of the anaphora, which has been taken into the South African rite—the words of administration. These are the same as the first half of the words of 1662 but with the curious omission of 'which was given/ shed for thee'. Certain papers among the records of the liturgical committee suggest that the form was derived from *Proposals*. These are undated typescript notes which passed between Dr. Phelps, the bishop of Grahamstown, and Dr. Baines, the bishop of Natal. A letter filed with the notes, signed by Phelps and dated 'Grahamstown, 1919', makes it clear that the notes are comments made by Baines on the *Alternative Form* of 1919. Phelps was chairman of the committee responsible for the printing of the form and seems to have sent Baines something in the nature of a rough draft as prepared for the printers. Baines's comments suggest that the draft had gone beyond the printing commission's terms of reference at several points. The commission had been doing its work largely, if not entirely, by correspondence. Phelps, as the bishop on the spot (for the form was printed by Grocott and Sherry of Grahamstown), would certainly have had to bear most of the responsibility for the details of the draft. On the form of administration Baines wrote:

Was not the alternative proposal here made [i.e. to have an invitation beginning 'Draw near and receive . . .' followed by the shortened words of administration] considered and rejected by [Episcopal] Synod? If so it is not in the power of the printing commission to consider it. The same, I think, is true if the proposal was not considered by Synod. [An almost indecipherable note in pencil in the margin seems to read, 'I thought rejected'.]

If however the majority of the printing commission do not agree with me then I would ask:

1. Whether in the new form of service the invitation [i.e. the shorter exhortation] as it stands in the Prayer Book has been omitted,

2. and, if it has not been omitted, whether the introduction of the words 'Draw near' in the alternative proposal is not open to the objection that they are a repetition of what has already been said?

Personally I should prefer the resolution of the Episcopal Synod, which was confirmed by the Provincial Synod of 1915, to stand, and to be included in a rubric at the end of the service.

In the event the alternative form of administration was not introduced into the South African revision until 1920. The 1919 form simply contained a rubric such as Baines had suggested. But the proposal to adopt the shorter words must have come from Phelps. Phelps had been a member of the Grahamstown group who had originally sponsored the *Proposals*. The shortened form proposed by Phelps and eventually incorporated into the South African rite is identical with that of *Proposals* as to the words of administration. The invitation is slightly different but is derived from the same material as that used in *Proposals*. The implications seem to be plain.

No other parts of the present rite can be traced to *Proposals*, but it is worth noting that the order of the various prayers in the final South African form is the same as the order proposed by Bazeley and Gould. It is a sensible and natural order, and that may be sufficient to explain its final adoption.

These few small points of similarity, most of them capable of being explained away, may be felt to be a very slight result for the labours and ingenuities of the authors of *Proposals*. But their real achievement lies elsewhere. Their view of the proper pattern for an anaphora shaped the official policy in revision over the whole period until the form was completed in 1924. The theories for which they argued so completely dominated the work of revision that nothing else managed to oust them, even if their own attempt to give those theories a practical application failed to be accepted by the Province at large. Their influence in originating the serious work of revision merits clear recognition and must never be underestimated.

CHAPTER THREE

THE FIRST OFFICIAL RITE

IN REPLY to the various criticisms that were made of their work in *Proposals*, Bazeley and Gould published a joint letter in the *Church Chronicle* towards the end of 1913. In it they said:

We have ventured to offer a detailed suggestion; but what we hope is that the Provincial Synod of 1915 will appoint a committee to receive and consider all suggestions and publish definite proposals before the ensuing Synod.

In point of fact the provisions made by provincial synod were, as has already been noted, very much more modest than the authors of *Proposals* might have hoped. One of the most significant implications of their letter is that even Bazeley and Gould were beginning to modify their earlier revolutionary attitude to the Prayer Book. It may be that the radical revision suggested in *Proposals* had provoked a reaction against any kind of change. The letter continues, at all events, in a surprising vein:

There is substantial agreement amongst liturgical students (i) that the preface, 'the prayer of consecration', the prayer of oblation, and the 'Our Father' should be reunited; (ii) that there should be some mention of the Holy Spirit; (iii) that memorials of the Resurrection, etc., are required by universal tradition.

In spite of the fact that this letter reiterates the main points of *Proposals*, it really represents a substantial concession to the school of thought represented by Dr. Frere. It is true that the writers maintained that without recognition of the principle that the consecration should be a prayer of thanksgiving arranged in logical order, 'no work can be satisfactory or permanent', but they seem to have come to realize that such a principle could be embodied in an anaphora far less revolutionary than that of *Proposals*. The first of their three points might have come straight from *Some Principles of Liturgical Reform*. In the second, 'some mention of the Holy Spirit' implies a very different thing from the invocation of *Proposals*.

What is happening, surely, is that Bazeley and Gould are beginning to compromise with the approach adopted by Frere and the South African bishops. The process of compromise, indeed, continued. Gould, in particular, came more and more to accept what might be called the 'Frere pattern' for the anaphora, until in 1927 he could write, in a memorandum addressed to episcopal synod, and now kept in the liturgical committee files:

The Prayer Book Measure [i.e. the proposed English rite of 1927] Prayer of Consecration is more logical, definite, beautiful and nearer to ancient precedent [than the South African]. . . . Still 'we offer here . . . everlasting salvation' is better than the corresponding phrase in the Prayer Book Measure. . . . Permission to sing *Benedictus qui venit* is a considerable gain [in the Prayer Book Measure]. . . . *Summary:* If the much better Prayer of Consecration is given due value the Prayer Book Measure will be preferred.

When this memorandum was written, the South African rite needed only the formal assent of provincial synod in 1929 to become fully canonical, and Gould was arguing that it would be better simply to take over the English Book of 1927 rather than to proceed with the ratification of the South African rite. Bazeley was probably less compromising, yet the letter which he had written with Gould in 1913, shows that there *was* at that early stage a 'substantial agreement' to which most of those desiring revision subscribed.

Less than a year after the publication of this letter, war broke out. Fortunately the revision of the Prayer Book in South Africa was not one of that multitude of pressing ecclesiastical matters to be shelved on the pretext that the war was engaging the entire energy of the Church. Nevertheless it was bound to have some effect upon the course of revision. Men's attention was focused elsewhere and the machinery of church government was inevitably slowed down. The forces working for revision remained surprisingly active but their activities made less impression upon the minds of their contemporaries.

After the publication of the bishops' second schedule, *Prayers upon Several Occasions*, in 1915, Frere's and W. C. Bishop's were not the only influences to be reckoned with. But unfortunately, as the situation becomes more complex, so the evidence upon which the history of revision is to be reconstructed becomes correspondingly more elusive. The records preserved in official archives cover this period only scantily.[1] A great many facts which ought to be established with ease are now merely a matter for hypothesis and conjecture, and even memory cannot always fill what sometimes seem to be quite obvious gaps. Priests of the Province who are now about the age of retirement, were not yet 30 when the serious work of revision was being done. Their knowledge of what was happening in the inner councils of the Church was not, in the nature of things, very great and it is astonishing how rapidly memory can fade. Thus no record of many events of the period now exists; other events can only be inferred from such records as have been preserved.

It is known that the liturgical committee must have received a copy of *Proposals*, since there is one among the records of the committee, but it is not known what the bishops made of the pamphlet. *Proposals* received a short notice in the *Church Chronicle* soon after it was published. Then nothing was done until the publication of the bishops' schedule of 1915, and after that no further move was made until *Proposals* was again reviewed in the *Church Chronicle* in the following year.[2] This time the reviewer was the Rt. Rev. W. E. Smyth, who had just retired as bishop of Lebombo to become rector of a parish in the city of Cape Town. Bishop Smyth's article reawakened the interest temporarily stifled by the war. Correspondence provoked by what he said continued until well into 1917. Not all those who wrote to the *Church Chronicle* desired extensive revision. A leading article in the early part of 1915 had condemned any attempt to forward an independent revision in any single diocese or province within the Anglican Communion, even in the 'mother' Church of England. The bishops' second schedule was praised as being within the competence of one Province; but the writer was of the opinion that independent provincial revision dare go no further.

Such caution was common in those who wrote in reply to Bishop Smyth's review. There were those who thought that there ought to be no revision at all lest it weaken the links with the Church of England. On the whole, though, it is astonishing how little evidence there is of rigid objection to any kind of revision at all. No doubt there was a great deal of silent conservative dis-

---

[1] See Appendix, p. 117.
[2] *Church Chronicle*, XIII, pp. 203 f.; and cf. Gould, 'The South African Liturgy', an article in the *Church Chronicle*, XXI, pp. 756 f.

approval, particularly among laymen. It would seem, for instance, that in the provincial synod of 1919 the whole body of lay representatives from the diocese of Cape Town were opposed to revision, but very little of this implacable opposition was vocal in the early days and this was probably partly because of the war. After the bishops' first *Alternative Form* was issued in 1919 there were public protests against the 'proposals to tinker with a part of the Prayer Book, which it is felt should be the most jealously guarded of all'.[3] And there was considerable, and very vocal, opposition in the provincial synod of 1919, led by T. J. Anderson of Sea Point in the diocese of Cape Town, who objected strongly to any kind of alternative to the Book of 1662. 'As to the alternative liturgy, he could conceive of nothing more pregnant with the seeds of disturbance and heartburning than that.'[4] The opposition seems to have found a good deal of sympathy and interest in the country at large. The East London *Daily Dispatch* for 11 November 1919 carried the following report:

The proposal called forth strong opposition. Mr. T. Anderson urged that going back to the old Prayer Book [1549] was merely a royal road to transubstantiation, and said it was a pity such a bone of contention should be thrown down at a moment when people were yearning for union.

After 1919 this opposition, with its fine command of outworn metaphor, seems to have died down, until in 1924 the final alternative form was approved, with only one dissentient. Apart from these few indications, there is hardly a trace of violent opposition to any revision of the liturgy at all. It has been thought worth collecting what evidence there is at this point (though it strictly covers the whole period and is not all immediately relevant to the early history of the revision) so that its extent could be measured and the scantiness of references to it could be appreciated.

The really widespread disagreement seems to have concerned not whether there should be a revision at all, nor even, particularly, whether the revision should be 'catholic' or 'protestant', but what particular type of ancient Christian model the new revision ought to follow. Quite apart from those who opposed revision, either because they feared it as 'Romanizing', or because it might weaken the links with the Church in England, there were four

---

[3] *Church Chronicle*, XVI, p. 350.
[4] *Church Chronicle*, XVI, p. 494.

different schools each working for a quite different kind of revision. There was the Grahamstown group inspired by the work of Bazeley and Gould. There was the episcopal synod following a more moderate policy. There were those who advocated a thoroughly 'Western' type of revision, and there were those who desired the retention of 1662 with provision for 'enrichment' rather than revision. These last differed little in practice from the bishops in aims and ideals.

The ranks of those who are opposed to Prayer Book Revision are swollen by the addition of many who feel very strongly that the Book of Common Prayer, as it stands, is the bond of union between many members of the Church, however much they may differ in private opinion as to certain matters which have not been defined as articles of faith.[5]

'Enrichment' was felt to be the answer. At one time, even, the liturgical committee was officially styled the Committee for Prayer Book Enrichment. The word was meant to convey a sense of improvement without alteration—if such a thing were possible. The article just quoted was one of a series written in the *Church Chronicle* during 1914 and 1915, specially to advocate enrichment as against revision. Some of its author's ideas as to enrichment are rather odd. In another article of the series he advanced a most peculiar scheme for the conflation of matins and the communion office, a liturgical exercise which seems to have been popular at the time. The service was to consist of matins up to the end of the second lesson, then the eucharistic liturgy, then the sermon, *and then the rest of matins*. Thus with very few changes of the Prayer Book text, the services could be enormously enriched. These articles would be likely to encourage the bishops, the more eccentric peculiarities apart, to stand firm on the position of the 1915 schedule and to resist the attempts of the Grahamstown group to achieve something more thorough. On the whole the bishops and the 'enrichers' were at one.

The 'Westernizers', too, had been advocating revision for some time. Like Frere they desired a reunion of the canon of 1549, but for rather different reasons. The Rev. W. T. Alston of Pietermaritzburg in Natal was the first public advocate of a scheme to make the Prayer Book approximate more closely to the Roman rite.[6] Alston assumed that the Prayer Book was essentially a part of the Western tradition and could only be revised within that tradition. He also assumed that the basic common order of the liturgy in East and West was: *Sanctus*, words of Institution, prayer for the communicants, Lord's prayer, communion, post-communion and dismissal. 1662 could be arranged to follow this pattern by analogy with the Roman rite as follows:

Hear us, O merciful Father	*Quam oblationem*
Who in the same night etc.	*Qui pridie*
Wherefore, O Lord, etc.	*Unde et memores*
Here we offer etc.	*Supplices te*
(A memento of the dead to be recited	*Memento*
secretly by the celebrant)	
And although we be etc.	*Nobis quoque*
Our Father	*Pater*
(Fraction and *Agnus* secretly)	*Libera nos* and *Agnus*
Almighty and everliving God, . . .	Post-communion
Peace and blessing	*Ite, missa est*

Alston's articles, though they stood alone as early public advocacy of Roman models, indicate that the outburst of later feeling in favour of 'the Western form of consecration' was not something new. Probably the Westernizers, like the conservatives, represented a large body of opinion, which was itself silent rather than vocal in its desire for its own kind of revision. Western influence was at its strongest in 1920 and 1921 but it already existed even before 1918.

Alston's articles did not, however, appear until the Grahamstown group had again begun to press for a more radical revision. Further pressure was brought to bear upon episcopal synod. Canon Gould, in a brief account of the history of the South African revision written in 1924, attributed the next move to a meeting of the sacred synod of the diocese of Grahamstown.[7] This view was commonly held, apparently. The *Newsletter*, magazine of the diocese of Grahamstown, in March 1918, said of the *Proposed Form* issued by the bishops in the same year:

At the last Synod of the clergy it was resolved that the Bishop be respectfully requested to approach the Bishops of the Province with a view to making certain changes in our Order of the Holy Communion so as to bring it into line with other liturgies of the Church. The result

[6] *Church Chronicle*, XIV, pp. 353, 376, 400.
[7] *Church Chronicle*, XXI, p. 756; and cf. *Historical Records*, p. 292.

has been the 'Proposed Form of the South African Liturgy' which is
now in our hands.

This simplified view of things, however, cannot be correct. The
time factor alone would have made it almost impossible for the
bishops, meeting in October 1917, to receive a request from the
Grahamstown synod which had met only a month or two
previously, to agree in principle to the whole idea of further
revision and draw up a detailed revised service, all on the spur of
the moment. Obviously the bishops had begun to plan some
further step beyond the schedule of 1915 even before they
received the request from Grahamstown. The minutes of the
episcopal synod, in any case, make it clear that Phelps, now bishop
of Grahamstown, had already prepared the way.

Phelps had become bishop in October 1915, just before the
bishops' second schedule was issued. He had been one of the
group which had sponsored *Proposals*. Like Bazeley, Phelps
suffered from crippling and almost continuous pain. He had been
hurt in a riding accident as a child and had been left with 'curvature
of the shoulder and a shortened leg'. Archbishop Lang once
referred to him as a saint, and it is as a saint that he is remembered
by a great many who served under his leadership. He loved small
children; and curiously, in spite of his hunch-back, children usually
loved him. He had come to South Africa to be chaplain to the
community of sisters in Grahamstown and it was this office which
he held at the time of the publication of *Proposals*.

Bishop Cornish showed wisdom by making Phelps Dean of Grahamstown when the vacancy occurred, in order that he might be better
known to the general public in the City and Diocese. Having thus
persuaded Phelps, much against his will, Bishop Cornish resigned his
See, and the elective assembly had no difficulty in choosing Phelps to
replace him.[8]

When he had been bishop for a little over a year Phelps
proposed at the session of episcopal synod held on 7 November
1916

that in view of the dislocation of the Canon of the Mass in the Book of
Common Prayer and of the unregulated and unsatisfactory custom
widely prevalent of the introduction as *secreta* of portions of other
liturgies, this Synod considers that individual bishops may rightly
sanction, under careful control and supervision, experiments which

[8] Pierce Jones, *Procession of Witness* (Cape Town, 1947), p. 21.

may result in the Church of the Province acquiring a Liturgical form of the Eucharist more in accord with Primitive models.

The proposal was seconded by Bishop Chandler of Bloemfontein. The influence of Bazeley and Gould's pamphlet is obvious, particularly in the phrases 'experiments which may result in . . . a Liturgical form . . . in accord with Primitive models'. The opposition to Phelps's motion was such that he asked leave to withdraw it. He and Chandler then substituted another proposal, which called for the appointment of a committee to discover exactly what powers episcopal synod had to revise the Prayer Book, to investigate the possibility of allowing some measure of experiment, and to devise some means of regulating interpolations from other rites. The very existence of this committee helped to make it possible for the bishops to accede to the request from the sacred synod of Grahamstown with the alacrity with which they did so.

By the time the sacred synod met, the correspondence and articles which had been appearing spasmodically in the *Church Chronicle* since Bishop Smyth's review of *Proposals* had reached considerable proportions. One of these articles, contributed by Gould and entitled 'The Revision of the Eucharistic Canon',[9] was later republished in pamphlet form for the special purpose of being circulated to the members of the sacred synod. The pamphlet is undated and bears no printers' name, but a short prefatory commendation written by Phelps is dated 1 July 1917. This commendation runs:

As the subject of the Revision of the Consecration Prayer is to be discussed in Sacred Synod, I am glad that this paper should be circulated amongst the clergy, as I consider it will help the Synod greatly in its consideration of the subject.

The article represents a considerable modification of Gould's views as found in *Proposals*. Gould had already prepared the way for such a modification by publishing an earlier article entitled 'A Western Anaphora',[10] in which he advocated the adoption of a consecration prayer like that of 1549, but with the invocation after the words of institution and with the addition of a memorial of the Incarnation. This so-called Western anaphora seems to have openly followed the pattern of the Gallican masses, for after the

---

[9] *Church Chronicle*, XIV, p. 212.
[10] *Church Chronicle*, XIV, p. 95.

Sanctus comes the *Benedictus qui* and then a passage running, 'Truly holy, truly blessed, is thy Son Jesus Christ Our Lord, whom Thou, O heavenly Father, of thy tender mercy didst give to become incarnate and dwell with men and to suffer death upon the cross'. This has a distinctly Gallican flavour.[11] The invocation of this anaphora was to be:

Humbly we pray and beseech Thee, Almighty God, pour out thy Holy Spirit upon us, that we receiving this Holy Communion in remembrance of the death and passion of thy Son, may be partakers of His Body and Blood and be fulfilled with thy grace and heavenly benediction.

It is noteworthy that Gould has here preferred an invocation upon the worshippers and not at all upon the elements.

Gould's later published article, *The Revision of the Eucharistic Canon*, circulated to all members of the synod, repeated, though very much more briefly, the main substance of the argument of *Proposals*. He was still moving towards a scheme of revision more sympathetic to the Book of Common Prayer, but he continued to base the theory of revision on W. C. Bishop's rationale of the primitive consecration prayer. Presumably because his article was popular rather than academic, Gould did not give detailed references to his sources until he came to deal with Anglican consecration prayers. The first Anglican recognition of the fact that the consecration prayer ought to be a prayer of thanksgiving, he finds in Thomas Brett's *Collection of Primitive Liturgies*, and this, he says, was not really followed up until W. C. Bishop began his work.[12] The defects in the 1662 form, as Gould saw them at the time of the writing of this article, were that there is no thanksgiving at all except in the preface (the prayer of Thanksgiving being specifically for *communion*), and that the consecration prayer is broken into fragments instead of following one clear, logical pattern.

---

[11] Cf. 'In the bulk of the Gallican post-sanctus prayers it is Our Lord who is spoken of as "Vere Sanctus".'—Frere on the South African *Proposed Form* in Jasper, *Walter Howard Frere*, p. 204.

[12] Bishop in *C.Q.R.*, LXIII, pp. 317 ff., LXVI, pp. 385 ff., and LXXX, pp. 359 ff. But there were others, in the seventeenth and eighteenth centuries, besides Brett, who recognized that the primitive consecration prayer was a prayer of thanksgiving. See Bingham (to whom Brett actually refers in the passage cited by Gould) in *Antiquities* (reprint of 1870), vol. II, pp. 770 ff., and also *N.B.* Thorndike's *Works* (Library of Anglo-Catholic Theology), IV, pt. I, pp. 52 ff., and see the lengthy anaphora of Stephens's *Liturgy of the Ancient Christians* in Hall, *Fragmenta Liturgica*, II, pp. 66 ff.

This part of Gould's *Revision of the Eucharistic Canon* is very much more like the sort of thing usually advanced by Frere than by Bishop. Gould indeed refers to *Some Principles of Liturgical Reform*, though without giving any specific reference. Again there seems to be an, at least tactical, acceptance of Frere's pattern for a revised anaphora in preference to the more elaborate pattern of *Proposals*. Gould cites as precedent for the longer 're-united' form of consecration, the 1549 rite and the Scottish rites of 1637, 1764, and 1910. He proceeds to a resumé of the Scottish and American consecration prayers and, again without specifically acknowledging his source, gives the rearrangement of the order of 1662 prayers advocated by Frere. Gould points out that a very similar rearrangement had been agreed to in the lower house of the Convocation of Canterbury. Finally he cites Cosin's well-known remark about Overall as evidence of a long-standing Anglican tradition that the prayer of Oblation ought to be said before the communion. This concludes his summary of the evidence in favour of a longer and fuller form of consecration than that of 1662. Gould adds to his article, with an amazing facility for producing anaphoras suitable to every occasion, a new proposed scheme for a revised South African consecration prayer.

Sanctus.
All glory and thanksgiving be to Thee, Almighty God our Heavenly Father . . . [continuing as 1662] . . . thine only Son Jesus Christ to become Incarnate and to suffer death . . . [as 1662] . . . in remembrance of me. Wherefore, O Lord and Heavenly Father, we thy humble servants, having in remembrance the blessed passion and precious death, the mighty resurrection and glorious ascension of thy dear Son, entirely desire . . . [as in 1662] . . . lively sacrifice unto thee; humbly beseeching thee to pour out thy Holy Spirit upon us, that all we who are partakers . . . [as 1662] . . . world without end. Amen.

This was the third order of consecration prayer to have been proposed by Gould and is even less revolutionary than his so-called 'Western anaphora'. It is of considerable importance in connexion with the *Proposed Form* of 1918.

By the time that the article containing this third anaphora was circulated to the clergy of the diocese of Grahamstown, a motion had already been set down on the agenda paper of the sacred synod requesting the bishops to permit

(1) the re-arrangement of the Holy Communion so as to go:

Preface; Sanctus; Consecration Prayer; Prayer of Humble Access; Communion; Prayer of Thanksgiving.

(2) the insertion of memorials of the great events in the work of our redemption such as are found in most other liturgies of the Church.

Bishop Phelps presided at the synod and there can be little doubt that he would have encouraged members to take a favourable view of the resolution. This was introduced by the dean, Bernard Williams, and seconded by the archdeacon of Port Elizabeth, A. T. Wirgman. Dr. Wirgman was a colourful and dynamic figure, the last colonial civil chaplain in the diocese. He was something of a liturgical scholar, having written, among a variety of other works, *The Prayer Book with Scripture Proofs*. The book has a quaint, old-fashioned flavour to the modern reader and the views expressed in it have no bearing upon the course of revision in this country. Wirgman's speech at the synod was almost his last official act, for he died soon after returning to Port Elizabeth.

The resolution seems to have met with general approval. According to the minutes of the synod, West, the chancellor of the cathedral and one of the Grahamstown group, seems to have spoken strongly in favour of the second part of the motion. He argued the necessity for a logical and straightforward anaphora for translation into the native dialects instead of perpetuating the defects of 1662.[13] Bazeley, now warden of St. Paul's, spoke too, reiterating his old argument that the 'do this' of the narrative of the institution must include 'give *thanks*'. Gould does not seem to have intervened in the debate at all and, although it cannot be definitely determined, it appears that he had already left the diocese to become a temporary army chaplain. It seems hard to explain, otherwise, why he should have kept silence on a matter for which he had done so much of the work. The motion was eventually carried with only two dissentients, and the request was forwarded to episcopal synod.

The bishops assembled for synod on 17 October. The report presented by the liturgical committee shows that the committee had been trying, not altogether successfully, to do its work by correspondence. Most of the report is concerned with prayers for the dead and is not relevant to the eucharistic anaphora. The only matter not irrelevant is the final statement in the report.

[13] Cf. *Proposals*, p. 16, where this point is made in almost identical language.

The report of the Joint Committee of the Convocation of Canterbury is in the hands of the Bishops; it deals with the reply of the Convocation to the Royal Letters of business. It contains matter of real liturgical interest, and it appears to be of urgent importance that the Synod should consider it, and determine the attitude to be adopted to it. It [this must refer to the Liturgical Committee] recommends that the Bishops should refer it [the Convocation report], with their recommendations, to their several Chapters, and that the reports of the Chapters shall be considered at the next meeting of the Synod.

Your Committee desire to draw attention to the new phase entered upon by the Lower House of Canterbury in regard to the dislocation of the Canon and trusts that the Synod will consider the subject afresh and arrive at some definite conclusion on this very important matter.[14]

It would seem, from the records of the episcopal synod, that the committee appointed as a result of Phelps's motion at the previous session of the synod had taken legal advice on the episcopal synod's powers of revision, for after the end of the meetings of the episcopal synod the archbishop, William Marlborough Carter, sent out a list of the proposed alterations to the Prayer Book, to which he appended a note:

I am not myself convinced by Chancellor Talbot that the fact that Provincial Synod might consider certain modifications in the Prayer Book Service to be for the general advantage of the Church of the Province constitutes 'a circumstance of this Province which requires modification'[15] of the Book of Common Prayer as we have received it from the Church of Engand. But assuming he is correct I should be prepared to sign the report.

Unfortunately it has not been possible to trace Chancellor Talbot's advice beyond this one reference, but the archbishop's letter makes clear that this legal advice had been sought and what the tenor of the reply was. On the other matter entrusted to it, the regulation of interpolations from other rites into the 1662 office, the committee was apparently able to do nothing.

The bishops in synod also received the request from the diocese of Grahamstown for thorough revision of the eucharistic rite.

[14] Report of the Committee on Liturgical Enrichment . . . to episcopal synod, 1917. The report from Convocation must have been Report No. 504, which was in fact later sent to the Chapters. The 'new phase' must refer to the move made by the Lower House of Canterbury to rearrange the order of the prayers in 1662 (see Jasper, *Walter Howard Frere*, pp. 58 ff.). Substantially the situation had not altered by the time the 1918 *Proposed Form* was produced.

[15] See *Constitution and Canons* (1950), p. 8; and cf. preface to the *Alternative Form* of 1919, p. 1.

The result of their deliberations on these various matters was that the synod decided it had the power, subject to the confirmation of provincial synod, to authorize departures from the Book of 1662, and it seems to have agreed in principle to the idea of revision and rearrangement. It appears to be unlikely, however, that the synod decided more than the principles, and perhaps the scope and extent of the revision. Probably the actual details of the revision itself were left to a committee appointed by the synod. The correspondence which passed between the archbishop and the other bishops suggests that the wording of the proposed departures from the 1662 Book had not been decided upon by the synod as a whole. Dr. Carter's letter was dated 23 January 1918 and read:

My Dear Bishop,

I am enclosing a copy of the resolution passed at the last Episcopal Synod for the rearranging of the Prayers in the Communion Office, and also the alterations. I am asking the Bishop of Grahamstown what he thinks should be done now with regard to arranging some copies of the service.

I should be glad to have your opinion in the matter. I don't suppose that there will be any demand for any large number of copies as yet, and perhaps it would not be as well to print the rubrics etc. Any suggestion from you would be helpful.

The meaning of the first paragraph of this letter seems to be that the synod had passed the resolution 'for the rearranging of the Prayers in the Communion Office', but not the actual 'alterations'. It was to this letter that the archbishop appended his note about Chancellor Talbot's opinion.

Phelps, as convener of the committee in charge of the revision, arranged to have copies of the service printed, and the bishops of the Province made no further comments or suggestions on the alterations proposed, for the printed *Proposed Form of the South African Liturgy* agrees exactly with the list appended to the archbishop's letter. Probably not many copies were printed, and certainly the use of the *Proposed Form* was very carefully controlled. In Grahamstown the Diocesan *Newsletter* for March 1918 announced: 'The Bishop has sanctioned the use of the new order at the Cathedral on two days a week, which days are Wednesday and Friday. Copies will be handed to those who come, or they can be purchased at 2d. each.' The bishop of St. Johns,

Dr. Williams, who had been Phelps's predecessor as convener of the liturgical committee, sent out copies of the *Proposed Form* to the clergy of his diocese with a covering letter dated May 1918.

The proposed form for a South African Liturgy is circulated for the information of Priests in Charge of Parishes. It is issued tentatively, and I shall be prepared to give permission for its use experimentally and occasionally in certain parishes in order that the people may become acquainted with what is proposed. It must not be used without the Bishop's expressed permission.

The new form, then, was altogether tentative and experimental, an indication of the sort of revision that might be attempted rather than a formal revision itself. It was, in fact, a 'proposed' rather than an 'alternative' form. This fact may help to explain why the bishops were content to decide the broad principle and leave the details to the committee. If the synod had already settled the details, there would surely have been no need for the archbishop some months after the synod had finished its sitting to circularize the members with copies of the report of the liturgical committee, and the details of the alterations proposed. In so far as the minutes of the synod are clear and decisive, they support this view. The report made by the liturgical committee in October 1917 contained no references to particular changes in the rite, but asks the bishops to consider the matter of revision and make it possible for their chapters to review the situation. Yet the archbishop attached to his letter a list of proposed changes headed 'Report of the Committee on Deviations from the Book of Common Prayer'. The report is not dated, but it is hard to believe that it had been presented in October 1917 at the same time as a report calling for general consideration of the whole question of revision. There was no other session of episcopal synod before the archbishop wrote his letter, so it seems that the committee must have produced the report containing detailed proposals for revision some time between October 1917 and January 1918, when the archbishop's letter was written. There would hardly have been time for the bishops to have drawn up the *Proposed Form* during the session of the synod itself. It seems far more likely that the course of events was something like this:

Episcopal synod met in October 1917 and received a report from the committee which drew their attention to Report No. 504 of Convocation and asked them to submit this to the diocesan chapters for consideration. But Report No. 504 contained no suggestions for revising the eucharistic liturgy, so the bishops were further asked to make some suggestions themselves on this part of the service.

The bishops did not draw up a detailed revised form for the liturgy at synod, for that would have left some unmistakable record in the minutes, but agreed in principle to the order of the rearrangement of the rite and referred the detail to the committee.

The committee drew up the *Proposed Form* between October 1917 and January 1918 and sent it to the archbishop, who circulated it among the bishops of the Province and then arranged to have it printed.

The *Proposed Form* was then issued for experimental use and submitted to the diocesan chapters for consideration.

The *Proposed Form* left the first part of the service untouched, though according to one of the schedules attached to the archbishop's letter, the committee had proposed to allow the summary of the Law or the threefold *Kyrie* to be used instead of the Decalogue. The form begins with the rubric, 'The service to the end of the Prayer for the Whole State of Christ's Church, as in the Book of Common Prayer. After which the Priest shall proceed, saying. . . .' Thereafter the order is:

Sursum Corda as in 1662
Preface and *Sanctus*
1662 Prayer of Consecration
Prayer of Oblation
Lord's Prayer
Short Exhortation, Confession, Absolution, and Comfortable Words
Prayer of Humble Access
Communion

This was not the order of prayers as requested by the sacred synod of the diocese of Grahamstown, whose proposed order agreed with that approved by the lower house of the Convocation of Canterbury.

The new anaphora, the basis of which was the 1662 prayers of Consecration and Oblation, contained several new phrases and clauses. It opened with the words 'All glory and thanksgiving be to Thee . . .', more or less what is found in the Scottish and American prayers. The rest of the 1662 prayer of Consecration was unchanged except for the addition of the phrase 'to take our nature upon him and . . .', from *Proposals*. The link with the prayer of Oblation was the customary 'Wherefore', almost invariable in Anglican revisions of the anaphora and suggested *inter alia* by Frere in *Some Principles of Liturgical Reform*. The *Proposed Form*, indeed, to a very large extent completed the work of remodelling the 1662 rite on the lines suggested by Frere in this book. The bishops' schedules of 1911 and 1915 followed Frere's pattern for revision. The *Proposed Form* continued the same policy and it was only, in the end, produced at all because the official reports of the English convocations contained no specific provision for a revised communion office. The fact that the *Proposed Form* is an application of the conservative scheme for revision suggested by Frere in 1911, makes Gould's acceptance of Frere's pattern for the anaphora a matter of considerable importance. Gould's influence on the 1918 form was very marked, as will be shown, but it could not have been so had Gould not already shown that he was willing to modify the revolutionary attitude that he and Bazeley had adopted in *Proposals*.

The prayer of Oblation in the 1918 form contains an anamnesis, 'having in remembrance the blessed Passion and precious Death, the mighty Resurrection and glorious Ascension of thy dear Son, and looking for his coming again with power and great glory'. These words are used in the Scottish rite and were borrowed from that source for the anaphora of *Proposals*. The 1918 form also contained an invocation, 'that thy Holy Spirit may be poured upon us that all we who are partakers of this Holy Communion may worthily receive the most precious Body and Blood of thy Son and be fulfilled with thy grace and heavenly benediction'. The words, 'may worthily receive the most precious Body and Blood of thy Son', are from the Scottish rite and had already been used in the invocation of *Proposals*. Otherwise, apart from the protocol introducing the Lord's prayer, the wording of 1662 is unchanged.

It is clear from the foregoing account that the bishops would be predisposed to accept these changes (whenever they were made by the liturgical committee), simply because they so very largely followed the suggestions made by Frere in *Some Principles of Liturgical Reform*, by which the bishops had already evidently been guided in their earlier attempts at revision. In this sense the *Proposed Form* merely completed a scheme on which the bishops

had already embarked. But in addition the changes would be likely
also to commend themselves to Phelps and the Grahamstown
group, since so many of them reflect the spirit of the *Proposals*.
Indeed in a very real sense Gould must be regarded as the author
of the 1918 *Proposed Form*. The new anaphora echoed almost word
for word the anaphora Gould had devised in his article 'The
Revision of the Eucharistic Canon', published first in the *Church
Chronicle* and subsequently circulated in pamphlet form to the
members of the Grahamstown sacred synod. The only additions
to Gould's form were the three phrases, 'to take our nature upon
him', 'looking for his coming again with power and great glory',
and 'may worthily receive the Body and Blood of thy Son', and
the first two of these are to be found in the anaphora of *Proposals*.
The one which refers to the Incarnation is happier than Gould's
later suggestion 'to become Incarnate' since it fits more easily into
the rhythm of the 1662 sentence. In all other respects Gould's
suggested anaphora and the anaphora of the *Proposed Form* are
identical.

It is not surprising that Gould's influence upon the new form
should be so strong. The order had been drawn up by a committee, which probably possessed considerable powers of independent
action, and of which Phelps was the convener. That Phelps was
still favourably inclined towards the point of view held by Gould
is evident in the commendatory note with which he prefaced
'The Revision of the Eucharistic Canon'. Moreover Gould had
considerably modified the plan for revision as first put forward in
Proposals. He was no longer demanding anything so revolutionary.
'The Revision of the Eucharistic Canon' is much more modest
and much more limited by the traditions of the Book of Common
Prayer. There is no doubt that Gould's later attitude would be far
more acceptable to the bishops as a whole, and 'The Revision of
the Eucharistic Canon' was prima facie more likely to influence
South African revision than was *Proposals*, even though it is a
much less significant and less well documented work than the
earlier pamphlet.

The impression that the 1918 *Proposed Form* was largely the
work of the Grahamstown group, and of Gould in particular, is
strengthened by the language of the preface to the *Proposed Form*.
The preface begins:

When Our Lord commanded us to 'Do this' He intended us to

include among those things to be done, not only the Breaking of the Bread and the directions 'Take eat' and 'Drink ye all of this' but also the Giving of Thanks, since that was the first step in his own action at the Last Supper.

This argument is so typical of Bazeley that the language might very easily be his. Again, the preface goes on to say:

The lack of thanksgiving in our present service has had the further result of obscuring the God-ward aspect of the Eucharist as a corporate act of worship, and has concentrated attention upon 'the altar rather than on the heavenly action; the Consecration seems to be the work of the Celebrant, to the exclusion of the offering Church' (Frere).

This quotation presents in summary form the spirit of the 1918 rite. That rite was almost certainly the work of the Grahamstown group, whose views in turn had by this time been considerably modified by those of Frere and had therefore become more generally acceptable to the province at large.

The preface ended by claiming for the *Proposed Form*:

I. that it contains the thanksgivings referred to above;

II. that it is much easier to explain, owing to the continuity of subject in each part;

III. that it makes clear the fact that corporate worship is an essential of the Eucharist;

IV. that it makes no change in the Doctrine of our Church since the significant phrases of the service remain unaltered.

It was at this point in the history of the South African rite that the two fundamental themes of *Proposals*—logical order and emphasis upon thanksgiving—became part of the anaphora. From 1918 it was the official policy of the revisers that the consecration should exhibit these two features, and undoubtedly it was Phelps who was the link between *Proposals* and the *Proposed Form*.

CHAPTER FOUR

THE FRERE PATTERN

A COPY of the *Proposed Form* was sent to Frere. It was probably Phelps who asked him for his comments on the form, though it is always a little difficult to tell for whom documents sent to the committee were intended. Since all the members of the liturgical committee at this time were bishops, letters which begin simply 'My dear Bishop' or 'My Lord Bishop' might have been meant for any of them. Phelps was convener of the committee, however, and it is probable that Frere's letter was sent to him in the first place. In the later stages of the revision of the South African Prayer Book Frere's contact with the liturgical committee was through the two bishops who had connexions with Mirfield, the head-quarters of Frere's community; Bishop Nash, the coadjutor bishop of Cape Town and a member of the community, and Bishop Talbot of Pretoria, whose brother succeeded Frere as superior of the C.R. In 1918, however, Talbot was not yet a bishop, and Nash had only just become one.

Frere addressed a memorandum, dated 1 August 1918, to the episcopal synod. It was a cyclostyled document of several pages, dealing in detail with the *Proposed Form*. The memorandum is printed *in extenso* in R. C. D. Jasper's *Walter Howard Frere*[1] and a copy is preserved among the papers of the liturgical committee. Frere's suggestions were that:

(1) The salutation should be restored to the *sursum corda*. [This was done in the 1919 *Alternative Form*.]

(2) In the Preface the words 'O Lord, Holy Father, Almighty Everlasting God' should read 'O Holy Lord, Almighty Father, Ever-lasting God.' [This has never been done.]

(3) In the *Sanctus* the form should run 'Holy, Holy, Holy . . . full of thy glory. Hosanna in the Highest. Blessed is he that cometh in the name of the Lord. Hosanna in the Highest.' [This, too, has never been part of any South African revision.]

On the third of these points Frere's argument was:

[1] pp. 203 ff.; and also in part in Arnold, *Anglican Liturgies* (Oxford University Press, 1939), pp. 189 ff.

The Hosanna, Benedictus and Hosanna repeat seem originally to have been taken from Ps. cxviii through the account of the triumphal entry to a place immediately before the Communion: and thence to have been transferred and brought into conjunction with the Sanctus. Thus they hold this position not only in the Roman rite but also in the Gallican, the Syrian, and the Byzantine. This being so, it seems highly desirable that they should be restored in our Order to that position. The only alternative is to end the Sanctus as it ended before this addition, viz. at the words 'Full of thy Glory'.

South African opinion on this point was divided. Gould, for example, had accepted the idea that the *Benedictus* should be restored, even before Frere wrote his memorandum, but Bazeley probably never accepted it.[2] In the event, the South African rite reflected Bazeley's view rather than Gould's; but that was probably owing to nothing more than to the consistent desire of the revisers to change as little of the people's part of the liturgy as possible.

Frere's next point is consequent upon his proposal to reunite *Sanctus* and *Benedictus qui venit*. It was:

(4) The prayer following the Sanctus ought, on the basis of parallels in the Gallican masses, to start 'Holy in truth art thou (and blessed in truth), O Almighty God . . .' (i.e. *vere sanctus, vere benedictus*). [This, too, had already been suggested by Gould in 1917 but has never been adopted, presumably because of the absence of the *Benedictus*.]

(5) In the Prayer of Oblation the invocation of the Holy Spirit should follow closely upon the mention of the second coming. [This suggestion was carried out in the 1919 form.]

(6) The offering of the gifts should follow some such form as 'Wherefore O Lord . . . glory, do offer unto thy Divine Majesty these sacred gifts and creatures of thine own, this holy bread of eternal life, this cup of everlasting salvation.' [This was incorporated in the form of 1919 and the phrase 'these sacred gifts and creatures of thine own' became one of the most bitterly contested points in the whole revision.]

(7) & (8) The Invocation ought to fulfil two conditions

    (a) that it should be explicit as to the reality of the consecration and should therefore contrast 'bread' and 'wine' with the consecrated Body and Blood, and

    (b) that it should do so in a way that avoided the controversy between East and West as to the moment or operative words of consecration.

Frere does not say how it is possible to have an invocation which

---

[2] *Theology*, II, p. 163.

fulfils both these conditions. Any form which contrasts strongly 'bread' and 'wine' with 'Body' and 'Blood' is almost bound to suggest that the change is taking place at the moment when those words are recited. Frere gave a great many examples of invocations most of them of the Gallican type, and he suggested two possible forms himself, neither of which really fulfils the two conditions which he had laid down:

May thy Holy Spirit descend upon these offerings and hallow this oblation of the Body and Blood of thy Son Jesus Christ Our Lord.

... entreating thee to send from high heaven thy Holy Spirit to sanctify our offerings and to hallow these our vows; that by the dew of his grace this mystery of the Body and Blood of thy Son may be available for the healing of our souls.

The phrase 'hallow this oblation' was part of the invocation of the 1919 South African form, but otherwise Frere's wording was not followed.

Frere made two last points:

(9) The Lord's Prayer ought to have some special eucharistic ending, either (a) the Doxology, which should then be removed from all other places where the prayer occurs, or (b) a prayer of the *Libera Nos* type. In the 1919 rite the Lord's Prayer was printed with the doxology but the prayer of Humble Access was adapted to serve as a *libera nos* prayer also. From 1920 onwards the second device was dropped—not surprisingly since the two suggestions are obviously alternatives—and the bishops adopted the other scheme, retaining the doxology here and omitting either it or the whole Lord's prayer wherever else it appeared in the Prayer Book.

(10) The Prayer of Humble Access might be made an 'embolism' to the Lord's Prayer by the addition of an opening phrase 'Deliver us from evil, and preserve us in all good, for we do not presume . . .'. Frere said, 'The suggestion has been made that the Prayer of Humble Access should be made a *Libera* Prayer . . .', and, in fact, the suggestion seems to have come from E. G. P. Wyatt's *The Eucharistic Prayer*.[3]

Frere also advocated that the penitential section of the service and the prayer of Humble Access (if it were not used as a *Libera nos*) ought to be removed from between the consecration prayer and the communion. He suggested that the translation of the *Gloria in excelsis* should be amended and that post-communion collects

[3] p. 63.

should be provided. But these were not matters affecting the anaphora.

The *Proposed Form* received very much rougher treatment from the Rev. W. Lockton in the *Church Quarterly Review*.[4] Lockton gave the bishops credit for neither courage nor originality. 'The revision', he said, 'seems to be based for the most part on the liturgy of the Scottish Church, though it is somewhat more conservative.' His critical attitude may possibly be explained by reference to another article of his appearing in the same number of the *Review*. This second article concludes with this judgement on the 1662 rite:

Consequently more than that of any other modern liturgy the method of consecration is in agreement with scripture and the most primitive practice of the Christian Church.[5]

Like the authors of *Proposals*, Lockton held that consecration was effected by thanksgiving, but unlike them he maintained that scriptural and apostolic traditions were against including an invocation in the anaphora.

In the meantime the bishops had referred the *Proposed Form*, together with Report No. 504 of the Convocation of Canterbury, to their chapters, as the liturgical committee had recommended. Since the Report did not contain any references to the eucharistic liturgy apart from the propers, the chapters of the dioceses of Cape Town, Grahamstown, and St. John's made very few recommendations on that part of the Prayer Book. A digest of the reports from these three dioceses, combined in one document and circulated to all members of the episcopal synod, is still in existence. There are a few suggestions touching other parts of the eucharist but none on the anaphora. Grahamstown asked for a new pro-anaphora, and all three chapters dealt fully with the prefaces and other propers. The most valuable reply, in a study of the history of the South African anaphora, came from the diocese of Pretoria. In those days this diocese covered the whole of the civil province of the Transvaal, and has since been divided into the two dioceses of Pretoria and Johannesburg.

There was, indeed, no chapter at all in that diocese and its functions were performed by the bishop's senate. Diocesan chapters in the Church of the Province have a curious and unique position. The dean is the only one of the canons who is a residen-

---

[4] LXXXVI, pp. 345 ff.   [5] p. 332.

tiary, and he acts as rector and parish priest. The bishop is the head of the capitular body and the bishop appoints the dean as he appoints every parish priest in the diocese. The archdeacons, too, are nominees of the bishop. The other canons, three or four in number, are elected in various ways, sometimes by the chapter itself, sometimes by the whole body of clergy in the diocese. The duties of the chapter are to advise the bishop in the administration of the diocese, rather than to govern the cathedral. In provincial and diocesan affairs the chapters have a recognized constitutional position and their members have a fixed place in the order of precedence of the Province. In the dioceses of Pretoria, Johannesburg, and Kimberley the bishop's senate replaces the chapter as a permanent diocesan advisory board.[6]

It was to a committee of the bishop's senate that the bishop of Pretoria referred Report No. 504 and the *Proposed Form*. This committee was appointed, as appears from the final report issued by it, on 13 November 1918. The committee consisted of seven clergymen with the Rev. Fr. Francis Hill, C.R., as chairman, and the Rev. G. H. Ridout as secretary. Ridout was probably the best liturgical scholar on the committee. 'That he could without warning take any part in any Christian rite . . . would certainly have been true of Ridout as regards Western rites.'[7] The committee's terms of reference were:

1. To make suggestions in regard to Prayer Book revision in South Africa.
2. To consider the question: Should there be a diocesan use, and if so, of what nature should it be?
3. To make suggestions for a new rite for Adult Baptism.[8]

The final report was a voluminous cyclostyled document reviewing the whole Prayer Book, and it amounted to a complete and independent scheme for revision. It followed the arrangement of Report No. 504, made detailed suggestions for every part of every service, and covered even those sections of the book not dealt with in the Report.

This immensely detailed review of the Prayer Book was submitted to Dr. Furse, the bishop of Pretoria. The report is dated 31 January 1919. The fact that the report was of such great

[6] Cf. *Historical Records*, p. 612.
[7] Pierce Jones, *A Procession of Witness*, p. 73.
[8] Report to the Lord Bishop of Pretoria, pt. 1 (31 Jan. 1919), p. 1.

length and was issued when the next session of episcopal synod was only a fortnight away, led the bishop to ask the committee to 'summarise the recommendations of their report and to suggest the best method of introducing to the Episcopal Synod the most urgent of the reforms recommended'.[9] Accordingly the committee met again on 13 February (only four days before episcopal synod was due to assemble) and issued a short second report recommending:

1. That a further modification of services for optional use be submitted to the next Provincial Synod of 1919 in the form of a resolution.

2. That a committee be appointed by the Bishops before the Provincial Synod of 1919, to sit for at least one week, for the purpose of drawing up this modification of services for optional use.

3. That the modification shall include:

(a) the order for the Celebration of Holy Communion;
(b) a revised form of the daily office;
(c) the Litany in a shortened form;
(d) Prayers and Thanksgivings.

The long first report had been issued far too late to affect the decisions of the episcopal synod, and, indeed, it covered a far wider field than the bishops were prepared to consider at that time. The real importance of the longer report lies in its effects upon events two years later in 1921, and even the second short report was not immediately effective. The only one of its requests to which the bishops acceded was the first one, which called for a further revision of the communion office; and even without this request the bishops would almost certainly have issued the revised form of 1919.

This revised form, the first *Alternative Form of the Order for the Administration of the Holy Communion*, was issued immediately after the session of episcopal synod had ended. For the first time in the history of the South African rite, revision covered the whole of the service. The order of the parts of the new rite was to be:

Lord's Prayer
Collect for Purity
Decalogue, Summary, or *Kyries*
Collect, Epistle, and Gospel
Creed
Offertory sentences

[9] Second Report to the Lord Bishop of Pretoria, 13 Feb. 1919.

Prayer for the Church (revised)

Short Exhortation, Confession, Absolution, and Comfortable Words

Sursum corda (with salutation and response), Preface, *Sanctus*

Consecration Prayer (extensively revised)

Lord's Prayer (with protocol and doxology)

Prayer of Humble Access

Communion (with provision for further consecration—in both kinds only)

Prayer of Thanksgiving (introduced by 'Let us thank God for his unspeakable gift')

Gloria in Excelsis

Blessing

This is the order that Frere had suggested in his memorandum to the bishops. It was also the order used by Bazeley and Gould in *Proposals*, and is the order of the present South African rite.

The principal source for the revision of 1919 was Frere's memorandum, 'Rough Notes on the Proposed Form of the South African Liturgy'. All the additions made to the anaphora were, with two exceptions, suggestions that had been made by Frere. The position and wording of the oblation and the phrase 'hallow this oblation' in the invocation were his. The two passages in the prayer not directly attributable to Frere were 'according to the institution of thy dearly beloved Son Jesus Christ'; and 'we humbly beseech thee to pour thy Holy Spirit upon us and upon these thy gifts . . .', the opening words of the invocation. Neither of Frere's suggestions for the invocation had been followed in full. It seems likely that what the bishops had done was to adapt the phrase just quoted from the Scottish rite and join it to Frere's phrase 'hallow this oblation'. The other passage not from Frere, 'according to the institution of thy dearly beloved Son Jesus Christ', appears in various forms in the Scottish, American, and 1549 rites, where it is associated with the words 'do celebrate and make here before thy Divine Majesty with these thy holy gifts, which we do now offer unto thee, the memorial which he hath commanded us to make . . .'. The omission of these clauses in the South African form certainly makes the prayer less clumsy. The Scottish form is again the probable model for the South African.

The liturgical committee had proposed that the anaphora should open with the words 'Holy indeed and Blessed art Thou, Almighty God our Heavenly Father . . .'. Presumably the committee was attempting to use the Gallican form of the *post-sanctus* without adopting the *Benedictus* on which it really depended. Frere had mentioned some instances of *vere sanctus, vere benedictus* being referred to the Father, notably in a Mozarabic mass for Easter,[10] though even in these instances the *Benedictus* had preceded this phrase. But episcopal synod rejected this particular suggestion from the liturgical committee, preferring the opening 'All glory and thanksgiving be to Thee . . .'. The bishops also instructed the committee to draw up an alternative form of confession and absolution and have it ready before the session of provincial synod planned for the end of the year.

The *Alternative Form* carried a preface which was to be the model for the prefaces of all future editions of the form. Its argument is arranged under five heads.

(1) The 1662 Book has been unchanged for 250 years and the need for revision has been widely felt throughout the Anglican communion. The desire for revision is perfectly consistent with an absolute loyalty to the standards of 1662.

(2) Legal advice had been taken and the Province has been said to be justified, under its constitution, in revising even where the reasons for revision are not exclusive to South Africa. Missionary work is one of the most pressing of all reasons.

(3) The Holy Communion is the great Thanksgiving of the Church. In the gospel accounts of the institution, and in the great liturgies, the giving of thanks is as important a feature as the breaking of the bread or the words of administration. More definite Thanksgiving helps to bring out the fact that the eucharist has a Godward side as an offering of a corporate act of worship and praise.

The other points in the preface are attempts to explain practical details of the revision.

The probability is that Phelps was the author of this preface. Reference has already been made to the correspondence which passed between Phelps and Bishop Baines of Natal in 1919. This correspondence quite clearly implies that Phelps had drafted the preface, which was later modified by Baines's criticisms.

Though W. C. Bishop's influence is still marked in the ideas expressed in the preface, the language of the anaphora of the 1919 form is derived almost entirely from the suggestions made by Frere. If the anaphora of 1918 had been virtually composed by

[10] Cf. Frere's memorandum in Jasper, *Walter Howard Frere*, pp. 204 f.

Gould, then the author of that of 1919 was certainly Frere. Almost without exception, the suggestions contained in his memorandum to the bishops were incorporated in the revised rite. The chief exceptions were the *Benedictus qui venit* and the cognate opening words of the prayer itself. It is even true to say that those parts of the prayer which had been taken over from the *Proposed Form* reflected the ideas of Frere, for Gould's anaphora, and the article in which he justified it, had been considerably influenced by Frere. The result is that in the 1919 form Frere's authority could be cited for almost every point at which the language differed from that of 1662. It was Frere's anaphora. The first *Alternative Form* was the high-water mark of Frere's influence upon the South African rite. Thereafter it tended to decline as the bishops made one concession after another under pressure of adverse criticism from the Province.

In July 1920 Frere reviewed the *Alternative Form* for the *Church Quarterly Review*.[11] Not altogether surprisingly, his attitude was extremely favourable to the new rite. The rite was, Frere said, 'a great advance upon the point reached by its predecessor and bids fair to provide the Province of South Africa with a worthy liturgy, and the Anglican Communion in general with a very valuable model'. Frere first gave a short account of the history of South African revision up to 1919 and then printed the new anaphora in full. Comparing this with the Scottish and American forms, he said:

The form of *anamnesis*, however, avoids the heaviness found in the Book of 1549 and followed by the Scottish Liturgy. . . . It avoids also any suspicion of a suggestion that some second action concerning the holy gifts takes place, over and above the one whole sacrificial action which is implied in consecration.

Frere complimented the revisers on the clarity and simplicity of the anamnesis and oblation, on bringing out the note of thanks-giving, and on the form of the invocation. On this last feature he wrote:

the position of the Anglican liturgies in regard to this matter is a question of momentous and practical interest. The compilers have surely been wise in following the guidance of Gallican rather than Greek precedents.

[11] XC, pp. 367 ff., reprinted in Alcuin Club Collections No. 35, *Walter Howard Frere*, pp. 123 ff.

Frere went on to repeat some of the things which he had already said in his memorandum to the bishops about the invocation and then passed to consider the matter which occupied most of his article, the method provided for a second consecration.

As the opponents of the 1919 form were later to make devastating use of the rubric providing for a second consecration—commonly known as the 'third rubric'—this matter is of great importance. The rubric ran:

If either the Consecrated Bread or Wine be all spent before all have communicated, the Priest having consumed whatever remains in the chalice, and having placed upon the Table new oblations of both Bread and Wine, is to consecrate in both Kinds according to the form before prescribed, beginning at *Hear us, O merciful Father* and ending at *Do this as oft as ye shall drink it in remembrance of me.*

Of this rubric Frere said:

it does not seem desirable henceforward to end with the words of Institution, as was necessarily done when those words ended the prayer. If a second consecration is needed, the ideal is that the whole Consecration Prayer should be repeated. If it is thought preferable that the whole should not be prescribed, it should be tolerable to begin with the second sentence . . . but the irreducible minimum should at least include the *anamnesis* and invocation.[12]

He went on to say, 'A second consecration is an expedient which in any case it is highly desirable to avoid'. In the place of a second consecration Frere advocated that when the consecrated wine was in danger of running out more should be consecrated by contact, either by pouring into it what was left of the consecrated element or by dropping in a fragment of a consecrated host.

The rubric in the 1919 form was indeed rather oddly framed. The words, 'the Priest having consumed whatever remains in the Chalice', provoked from Baines the comment, 'How can the Priest consume whatever remains in the Chalice if all be spent?'[13] The intention of the rubric clearly was that reconsecration should always be in both kinds. The awkward wording is easily explained. In order to comply with the terms of the rubric, any remaining consecrated wafers might be set on one side while one or two new ones were blessed with the chalice, but it would be more difficult to do the same thing with the wine without emptying the chalice

12 *C.Q.R.*, xc, p. 371.
13 Notes passing between Bishops Phelps and Baines now in liturgical committee files.

first. Since there were, apparently, those who, like Frere, held that wine could be consecrated by contact, simply refilling a chalice in which there remained even the smallest quantity might have led to all sorts of complications. A further reason for directing the priest to empty the chalice might be that, while it is probable that if the consecrated bread is spent it will all be spent, it is very difficult to ensure that the chalice is ever completely emptied by the communicants. There comes a point at which there is hardly enough left in the chalice to communicate anyone normally and properly, yet some small quantity of the consecrated wine remains.

Baines's protest did not prevent the rubric being printed in the *Alternative Form*. Bazeley and Gould in *Proposals* had directed:

If a re-consecration is required, let the Priest consecrate in both kinds, according to the form prescribed beginning at 'Our Saviour Christ . . .' and ending at '. . . all other benefits of his passion'.

Here is the same insistence upon a second consecration being in both kinds. The *Proposed Form* of 1918 had said, more ambiguously:

If the consecrated Bread or Wine be all spent before all have communicated, the Priest is to consecrate more according to the Form before prescribed beginning at [Our Saviour Christ in the same night . . .] for the blessing of the Bread; and at [Likewise after Supper . . .] for the blessing of the Cup.

This is, of course, the rubrical direction as it stands in the Book of Common Prayer of 1662, even to typographical details. It is ambiguous in the *Proposed Form*, because, although the consecration prayer in that form was followed immediately by an anamnesis and invocation with the 1662 prayer of Oblation, yet there is no direction to the celebrant where to stop when reconsecrating—unless the *Amen* after the words of institution was regarded as a sufficient indication. The probability is that the printers were simply given a copy of the 1662 Book to follow in those parts of the service not specifically affected by the *Proposed Form*. And in the 1918 form there was no direction to reconsecrate in both kinds.

Besides his criticism of the rubric on reconsecration, Frere's article included some remarks on the pro-anaphoral part of the new rite and compared the South African form of 1919 with the American Second Report of the same year. He had one or two suggestions for further revision. The most important was a repetition of his earlier plea for the 'recovering of the long mistranslated and truncated *Sanctus*'.[14] But Frere's influence had already reached its zenith. The 1919 rite represented the full flowering of the ideas Frere had been advocating since as early as 1911. With the publication of the first *Alternative Form* there began a gradual growth of open and vocal discontent with the 'Frere pattern' of the anaphora among the clergy of the Province.

[14] *C.Q.R.*, xc, p. 373; cf. Frere's memorandum (1918).

CHAPTER FIVE

THE EPICLESIS CONTROVERSY

THERE WERE those in the Province who argued that the invocation of the 1919 form made nonsense of the whole consecration prayer. The two phrases 'these . . . creatures of thine own' and 'hallow this oblation' were the centre of the controversy.

The difficulty is caused by a very natural desire to graft an Eastern or Greek Epiklesis upon a Western or Latin rite. . . . The difficulty is this. The Greeks in the plainest possible way make known by the form of their service that the Consecration takes place immediately after the Epiklesis; while the Latins make it equally clear that the Consecration is effected by Our Lord's own words. . . . Now in our 'Alternative Form' the 3rd rubric after the Lord's Prayer[1] makes it clear that the Consecration takes place by the recitation of those words of Institution. . . . The question before the Compilers of our 'Alternative Form' was this, Is it possible to combine with this a Greek Epiklesis? It was possible; and it was done, let us say, by Archbishop Cranmer and his Committee in the First English Prayer Book. He did it by putting *his* Epiklesis *before* instead of *after* the words of Institution. . . . There was no need to use the word 'creatures' [in the invocation] at all. But our 'Form' uses it twice in the same Prayer: and far, far worse actually after the Consecration [institution-narrative]. . . . But it may be said that the Consecration is effected not only by the words of Institution already recited, but by those words and the Epiklesis combined. I answer: No one can say this while Rubric 3 confronts him on the 'Form'.

These remarks were part of a paper 'read at St. Bede's College, Umtata, on January 8th, 1920, by the late Warden of the Society of Sacred Study at the Annual Meeting of this Society in the Diocese of St. John's'. The name of the speaker is not recorded, but he could have been no other than Canon J. E. W. Mason, warden of St. Bede's, a theological college for African ordinands. Canon Mason was warden of the society, too, until he retired from St. Bede's early in 1921. The diocese of St. John's corresponds in geographical area with the Transkei, an African reserve, and is, therefore, very much a missionary diocese. The

---

[1] i.e. the rubric laying down the form for a second consecration.

clergy would have included a large number of Africans, some of whom would have been trained by Canon Mason. Mason's paper was cyclostyled and circulated after his retirement, under the title quoted above. The fact that he is referred to as the 'late' warden in this title means that the paper was not 'published' until about a year after it had been delivered. That it should have been thought important enough to revive after so long an interval, together with the fact that at the time when it was delivered Mason occupied an official academic post of some distinction in the diocese, suggests that it was regarded as an authoritative, scholarly pronouncement and was well received in the diocese.

Canon Mason's views are quoted here, though out of strict chronological order, because they are typical of the argument used against the 1919 form. This argument became, in its essentials, the argument of all those who opposed the revised rite, but Mason presented it in its most concise and simplest form. The validity of the argument will be considered when the 'Natal petition', the most scholarly and important of the attacks on the 1919 form, is dealt with. At this point it is enough to say that the argument from the 'third rubric' breaks down because the bishops specifically directed that the celebrant in 're-consecrating' was to begin at 'Hear us, O merciful Father . . .'. In this they could be accused of inconsistency, but not of believing that the words of Institution were *alone* necessary for consecration.

The diocese of St. John's was not, of course, the only one which produced persons or groups who reacted strongly against the new 'South African Liturgy'. Indeed a great many people refused to allow it to take that name at all. Dr. J. T. Darragh, one of the most hostile critics of the form, wrote to Frere in 1921, saying:

I do not know how you came to consider it as a 'South African Liturgy', duly accepted and agreed upon. It is most certainly not so accepted and agreed upon, and is no more than a tentative and experimental document. There is not the least likelihood of its being generally received in the Province without some amendment of the language of the second Epiklesis.[2]

It must be remembered that Darragh said this after provincial synod had, at the end of 1919, 'discussed in detail . . . and adopted' the form. One wonders what was said of it before it had received

---

[2] Jasper, *Walter Howard Frere*, p. 212. Darragh, of course, reckoned 'Hear us, O merciful Father . . .' as the 'first Epiklesis'.

even that measure of formal recognition. Darragh also wrote, to much the same effect, to the editor of *Theology*, who reported:

The Revd. J. T. Darragh writes from Durban, S.A., to point out that strictly speaking the South African Liturgy, to which allusion has been made in our pages more than once, does not exist. There is a draft before the Province, which is not likely, he says, in its present form, to meet with the final approval of the authorities. . . . Mr. Darragh's letter was written before our March number appeared and his point tallies exactly with what Mr. Bazeley writes in the Lambeth Conference Review there published.[3]

As one of the things that Bazeley had said in his article was that the 'less learned dislike' the South African invocation 'as destructive of the ultra-Roman doctrine of Consecration by the words of Institution which is commonly taught among High Churchmen',[4] it is unlikely that Darragh's point tallied with Bazeley's quite as exactly as the editor rather ingenuously declared.

The most important effect of the publication of the *Alternative Form* of 1919 was that it brought the whole matter into the open for the first time. Hitherto it had been somewhat eclipsed by the war and by the rejoicing over the armistice of 1918. Indeed, one angry critic of the new rite, the Rev. M. O. Hodson, wrote, 'No doubt it is unavoidable, but at present the movement for revision resembles a knot of conspirators talking in a corner of a dark room'.[5] Hodson, who was later to be one of the leaders of the 'Natal petition' group, roundly condemned the 1919 form as a failure, and appealed for wider latitude in experiment. Other voices were now raised against the rite. Bloemfontein was the next diocese in which unhappiness about the revision made itself felt. Dean Hulme of Bloemfontein made a public plea for the transfer of the invocation from its place after the words of Institution to before them. The reasons for desiring the change the dean gave as being:

(*a*) that was the position of 'Hear us, O merciful Father' in 1662;
(*b*) that was also the place of the fuller invocation in 1549;
(*c*) the order of Our Lord's actions as recorded in the Gospels and in Corinthians in (1) taking the elements, (2) blessing or giving of thanks, (3) breaking the bread, (4) saying, 'This is my body'.

[3] *Theology*, II (April 1921), p. 208. Bazeley's article was a review of revision in the Anglican Communion generally.
[4] *Theology*, II (March 1921), p. 163.
[5] *Church Chronicle*, XVI (1919), p. 269.

The third of these points must mean that Dean Hulme thought of the invocation as the equivalent of 'blessing' and that it ought, therefore, to precede the fraction in the manual acts and the words of Institution. But later he was to interpret the invocation as meaning something very different. Plainly, however, at this stage Dean Hulme found the position of the 1919 invocation unsatisfactory.

Later, when the bishop of Bloemfontein (Chandler) had resigned and Hulme was vicar-general administering the diocese during the interregnum, a great deal of criticism of the invocation was ventilated in the *Church Chronicle*. Hulme wrote again, this time to defend the invocation, giving an explanation of it which he claimed to have received from his old bishop:

So in our new Liturgy, consecration is taken as effected through the recitation of the Narrative of Institution and Our Lord is sacramentally present, we then *later* ask the assistance of the Holy Spirit that we may worthily present Him—the Lamb—to the Father. It is an extension of the preceding phrase 'we offer . . . unto thy Divine Majesty'.[6]

This explanation is interesting for its bearing upon the theology of the bishops, but as an interpretation of the invocation it was unsatisfactory in every way. It did not satisfy those who objected to the invocation, for it did not explain the word 'creatures' coming after the narrative of the institution. Nor did it satisfy those who defended the invocation. One would have thought that, in any case, the plain sense of the language was against such an interpretation. Hulme's explanation equated the word 'oblation' with the word 'offer' in the preceding clause. The invocation was thus seen as a blessing not of the elements, but of the *act* of offering. The phrase 'hallow this oblation' was, however, certainly interpreted by most people, whether in support of the new rite or in criticism of it, as meaning 'make this gift holy for us', and therefore as a part of the form of consecration. The Natal clergy went so far as to say, 'We cannot be meant to be guilty of the impiety of superadding a consecration upon a consecration'.[7] The authors of the phrase certainly thought of it as being in some way consecratory. Bazeley attributed the whole of the invocation to Frere,[8] but in this he seems to have been mistaken. Frere's suggestions for the invocation have already been given, and one

[6] *Church Chronicle*, XVII (1920), p. 231.   [7] *Considerations*, p. 5.
[8] *Theology*, II, p. 163.

of these suggestions underlies the phrase 'hallow this oblation' which caused most of the trouble. Of the phrase Frere wrote:

The compilers . . . have good precedent behind them when they describe the Holy Spirit's outpouring upon the gifts in such a simpler reticent and non-controversial phrase as 'that he may hallow this oblation'.[9]

Frere, then, approved, though he did not entirely frame, the 1919 invocation, and clearly Frere understood the phrase 'hallow this oblation' (which *was* his own contribution) as referring to the work of consecration, though not necessarily defining the moment of consecration. The words 'the effect of the invocation' or other similar language is repeated again and again in his comments on the 1919 form. It is true that he does not specify exactly what this effect is, indeed he advocates 'reticence', but clearly he does not mean that the work of the Holy Spirit is confined to sanctifying man's *act of offering* to God.

The word 'oblation' may have many meanings in the liturgy. In the rite of 1919 it is used in the rubric regulating a second consecration to describe the unconsecrated 'oblations' of bread and wine. The preface to the rite refers to the 1662 'Prayer of *Oblation*' as now forming part of the consecration prayer, but the 'oblation' of the 1662 prayer is an offering of 'ourselves, our souls and bodies'. Nowhere is the word 'oblation' used of our act of offering of the Body and Blood of Christ, which is what Dean Hulme's interpretation meant. It is true that the preface to the rite says that 'we must first present Christ and His merits . . . then present ourselves trusting in the merits of our Head . . .', so, without doubt, the idea of some such offering was present in the meaning of the word 'oblation', but the word is never used elsewhere exclusively in this sense.

It would seem that Hulme later realized that his attempt at justifying the 1919 invocation was unsatisfactory, for in 1921, after the Natal clergy had petitioned against the form, he gave permission for all the priests in the diocese of Bloemfontein, of which he was vicar-general, to omit the two offending phrases. Thus there came into existence a variant of the 1919 anaphora, sometimes grandiloquently referred to as the 'Bloemfontein use', which anticipated the bishops' final solution to the controversy. Hulme's own account of his action was:

[9] *C.Q.R.*, xc, p. 370.

May I state that I am practically responsible for the particular *words connected with the consecration* as now used? . . . Perhaps our South African Bishops thought that . . . they would follow their two sisters [Scotland and America] and adopt an Eastern form of Consecration. So *suddenly*, in 1920, they issued a liturgy which, after what the Western Church had considered the words of consecration they went on. . . . 'We offer here unto thy Divine Majesty (these sacred gifts and creatures of thine own) this holy bread of eternal life, and this cup of everlasting salvation; and we humbly beseech thee to pour thy Holy Spirit upon us, and upon these thy gifts (that He may hallow this oblation and) that all we who are partakers of this Holy Communion may worthily receive. . . .' . . . Now I happened to be vicar-general at the time . . . and I authorised the omission of these words, in the quotation, just given, I have placed in brackets. . . . Thus there was no alluding to the *Consecrated Species* as Creatures; and there was no talk of hallowing the *already hallowed*; and the purpose of the Holy Spirit's co-operation was that we should 'worthily receive', i.e. make a good communion. . . . What as vicar-general I granted the Bloemfontein clergy has, since 1921, been adopted as the use of the whole Province.[10]

Hulme had, in fact, ceased to regard the invocation as a blessing of the elements or even of the act of offering. It was for him no more than a blessing of the reception. His attempts to explain the invocation contradict each other and are not, in themselves, easy to follow, but all this unhappy fumbling is evidence of the distress caused by the invocation. A great deal of the criticism of the *Alternative Form* was caused by this one fact.

When provincial synod met in November 1919 and the form was presented to it for approval, synod contained, in addition to the evangelicals who disliked any kind of revision at all, a large body of the clergy who were highly critical of certain features of the bishops' proposals. The preliminary agenda of the synod contained the item:

The Archbishop of Cape Town will move 'that this Synod expresses general approval of the revised liturgy and hopes that before sanctioning it as an alternative form for optional use in the Province, the Bishops will take counsel with representative men of the other orders of the Synod, in order that relevant criticisms and objections may be fully and carefully considered.'

The archbishop's unhappiness at the idea of revising the form at all has been already noted. The form which the notice of his

---

[10] Hulme, *Blackwall to Bloemfontein* (S.A. Church Publications, 1950), pp. 220 f. The italics are mine.

motion took clearly indicates that the bishops as a whole were not hopeful of piloting the 1919 form through the synod in its original shape. Since synod was unable to amend, the only method the bishops could employ to get their proposals passed in the face of the opposition was to frame some such motion as this so that members of the synod would be able to vote for the *Alternative Form* in principle, while hoping, at the same time, that it might be revised in certain details. The bishops were relying upon the support of those who, however unhappy they might be about the invocation, were delighted at the prospect of a revised rite in general. In spite of the bishops' apprehensions, the archbishop's motion was carried and the form received 'general approval'. That the margin of support for the proposals was of the very narrowest is indicated by the telegrams Gould received from Phelps and Bazeley. Gould was not a member of the provincial synod of 1919 but Bazeley was a representative of the clergy of the diocese of Grahamstown, and Phelps as a diocesan bishop was a permanent member of the synod. The telegrams, sent on 11 November 1919, were:

GENERAL APPROVAL OF LITURGY PASSED SYNOD YESTERDAY MAJORITY OF THREE IN LAY HOUSE LAUS DEO PHELPS GENERAL APPROVAL GIVEN TO LITKRYW [SC. LITURGY] VOTING BY ORDER BAZELEY

Provincial Synod normally votes by acclamation.[11] A division may be taken if any one member of the synod is dissatisfied with the president's ruling as to whether 'the Ayes or the Noes have it'. The rule for 'voting by order' is that it must 'be demanded immediately *before* the question is finally put' (that is, before any vote by acclamation is taken: this method of voting cannot be used to defeat something which has already been carried by acclamation and division). This manner of voting is only likely to be demanded when it is known beforehand that the majority either way is likely to be a narrow one, and when the matter is highly contentious. When the vote is taken, the bishops, the other clergy, and the laity vote as three separate houses and the motion must be carried in each house. The 1919 *Alternative Form* received general assent in each house, but in the house of the laity the majority was only three.

Synod also availed itself of the opportunity provided in the

---

[11] *Constitution and Canons* (1950), p. 178.

archbishop's motion to elect 'three members of each house to act as Assessors with the Bishops in the work of the Revised Liturgy'. The six assessors included Bazeley and Fr. Francis Hill, chairman of the Pretoria committee. It is almost impossible to say what influence, if any, the assessors had upon the shaping of the South African rite. They met with the liturgical committee immediately after the end of the session of provincial synod and reviewed the 1919 form. Further amendments to it were suggested. There is a scathing letter from Gould among the papers of the liturgical committee which suggests that the assessors were not particularly well qualified for liturgical work, though he expressly exempts Bazeley from this charge.[12] Gould even doubted, and he expressed his doubts in the same letter, that the assessors had ever met. But he is clearly wrong about this, since the official report on the work done in episcopal synod in October and November 1919 reads:

The proposed alterations in the Alternative Communion Office suggested at the conference between the Liturgical Committee and the Assessors elected by the clergy and laity of the late Provincial Synod were discussed in detail and the form as amended was adopted [adopted, that is, by episcopal synod].[13]

There is, in St. Paul's College library, a copy of the 1919 form with 'Suggestions for further revision' made in Bazeley's quite unmistakable hand. The copy certainly belonged to Bazeley at one time, for it was given to the college by his widow, but the manuscript additions are not dated in any way. It is just possible that these 'Suggestions' were in some way connected with the work of the assessors, for there would have been no purpose in Bazeley's making notes for further revision in a copy of the 1919 edition once the meeting of the assessors had been held, for that edition was almost immediately superseded by the revised (1920) form. If these suggestions of Bazeley's were connected with the work of the assessors, they had but little influence upon the changes made in the form. One of them, which has become a part of the final South African rite, was a proposal to omit the words 'militant here in earth' from the bidding before the prayer for the Church. Bazeley's suggestions for revising the anaphora were:

(1) to alter 'who made there (by his one oblation of himself once

---

[12] Letter from Canon C. J. B. Gould to the convener of the liturgical committee, dated 3 June 1933.
[13] *Church Chronicle*, XVII, p. 9.

offered) a full . . .' to read 'who by his own oblation of himself once offered made a full . . .';

(2) to alter 'a perpetual memory of that his precious death' to read 'a perpetual memorial of that his precious death and sacrifice';

(3) to omit 'Hear us, O merciful Father, . . . Body and Blood' and to begin the narrative of the institution 'For in the same night . . .'.

The first of these amendments was made in the revised form of 1920.

Episcopal synod, then, received the suggested amendments agreed upon by the six assessors and the liturgical committee. The bishops had already assembled once before, earlier in the year, to issue the 1919 form. They now met again, in October and November of 1919, before and after the session of provincial synod.[14] The minutes show that the revised rite was considered on 25 November. Phelps proposed the new amendments which had come from the assessors. The bishops adopted the amendments and so the *Alternative Form* of 1919, approved in principle by provincial synod on 10 November, was superseded in just over a fortnight by the revised edition of 1920.

As they affect the anaphora, the amendments of November 1919 are trifling. When the revised form had been published Gould wrote, 'Not a letter, not a point, has been changed in the most criticized passage, the anamnesis and invocation'.[15] The form as a whole differed from its predecessor in several details. The salutation and response were inserted before the collect; the words 'militant here in earth' were omitted before the prayer for the Church. The prayer of Humble Access was restored to its original form. 'Unimportant changes', Bazeley wrote, 'may provoke more opposition than important ones—e.g. the attempt to make the Prayer of Humble Access an *embolism* was most unpopular and the Bishops wisely removed the connecting words. . . .'[16] There had undoubtedly been a great deal of opposition to this use of the prayer of Humble Access.

In our Alternative Form the priest is ordered to kneel down and say 'Deliver us from all evil for we do not presume to come etc.' This repetition of the final petition in the Lord's Prayer is borrowed from the Sarum and Roman missals: but it does not fit the place in our

---

[14] For references to the proceedings of provincial synod, see the *very brief* account in *Historical Records*, p. 292, and Gould's remarks in *Church Chronicle*, xxi, p. 756.
[15] *Church Chronicle*, xvii, p. 155.
[16] *Theology*, ii, p. 162.

'Alternative Form'. The position differs greatly. In these Latin services the final petition . . . is made as a response by the people. The priest in a low voice says the Amen and proceeds 'Libera nos etc. . . .' an expansion of the petition and inaudible by the people. It is natural for the priest to say that petition for himself, which, as yet he has not spoken with his own mouth. But all that is foreign to our 'Alternative Form'—where the words 'Deliver us from all evil' are tacked on to 'the Pr. of humble access'—something quite different. It sounds like what it is—a patch.[17]

In the anaphora the word 'there' before 'by his one oblation' was omitted and the word 'made' was transferred to immediately before 'a full, perfect . . .'. The reason for this alteration was probably that the insertion of the words 'to take our nature upon him' had already made the eucharist a less narrow memorial of the passion alone and had made the word 'there' somewhat incongruous. The only other change was the restoration of the phrase 'to accept this our sacrifice of praise and thanksgiving . . . beseeching thee', following the usage of the Scottish and American rites. These words had been attached to the anamnesis of the *Proposed Form* of 1918 when it had been fitted into the prayer of Oblation. In 1919 the anamnesis had been replaced by a new anamnesis, oblation, and invocation, and the 1662 phrase had disappeared with it. After 1919 the anaphora was not altered again, except in one important particular to be noted later. Since that date the order of the prayer in the South African rite has been:

(1) the 1662 prayer of Consecration with a very few alterations,
(2) the anamnesis, oblation, and invocation (including two clauses from the 1662 prayer of Oblation),
(3) the rest of the prayer of Oblation.

The shortened form of administration was included in the 1920 edition of the rite. The rubric on second consecration was left unchanged.

The movement for revision in England was at this time rather behind what had been achieved in South Africa. In 1918 the archbishops had been requested to call a conference to discuss the deadlock reached in rearranging the canon. A rough draft of the initial recommendations of the committee was sent to Frere in May 1919.[18] The final proposals from the conference were sub-

---

[17] Paper read to the Society of Sacred Study, diocese of St. John's, by Canon Mason (see above).
[18] Jasper, *Walter Howard Frere*, p. 76.

mitted to convocation on 11 February 1920. As the South African anaphora had been settled by the time of the session of episcopal synod on 17 February 1919, there can be no question of any direct dependence on the English revision of 1927-8. The only part of the anaphora to be revised in South Africa after 1919 was the invocation; and that bears no real resemblance to the corresponding part of the Communion Office of the Deposited Book. Most of the similarities between the English and the South African revisions are to be explained as resulting from a common parentage in the ideas and circumstances which shaped the two rites. There were some incidental borrowings—for example, the South African rubric on the use of the Decalogue was taken from the English revised book—but none of them affected the consecration prayer.

The preface to the South African revised edition of 1920, 'Notes on the Revision of the Order for the Holy Communion', was reprinted exactly as it had stood in the 1919 edition, but with the addition of one short new paragraph which explained why it was fitting that the Lord's prayer should conclude the anaphora—'for it gathers up, in the highest form, all that has been prayed for therein'.

In spite of the gathering strength of the opposition, then, the changes made in the *Alternative Form* after the provincial synod of 1919 were very slight, and did not in the least affect the rationale of the order as set out by the bishops in their preface. The reluctance of the provincial synod, the smallness of the majority in favour of the rite, the representations of the assessors, all failed to make the bishops materially alter the form of 1919. Probably the bishops were hoping to be able to have the form again approved in the next session of provincial synod in 1924. For this it was essential that there should be no 'material alteration'. After the excitement in the synod itself, the whole matter seems to have dropped out of public notice. It is extraordinary, for instance, that the official report of the proceedings of the provincial synod printed in the magazine of the diocese of Grahamstown, makes no mention of liturgical matters at all. The matter is made to appear all the more odd by the fact that Phelps himself, in the same issue of the magazine, commented on the passage of the 1919 form through the synod.

The Revised Form received general assent. Further amendments have been made and it is to be printed and published as soon as possible. The Bishops passed a resolution that the Revised Form is only to be used where the Minister and people agree in desiring it. When the form is finally issued application must be made to me first for its trial as an experiment and then, if desired, for more regular use.[19]

Earlier in the year the bishop had authorized the use of the (unrevised) 1919 form on four successive Sundays (in the Cathedral these were 10 August and the next three Sundays), at the same time withdrawing the permission he had given for the use of the *Proposed Form* of 1918. Both these were now replaced by the guarded permission to use the 1920 form when it should have been published. It would appear that the bishops were hoping to overcome the opposition to the new form by exercising a great deal of tact in regulating its use so that it might be preserved unaltered to become finally canonical in 1924.

It was soon made clear to the bishops that the dissidents were not to be appeased by the few small changes to the edition of 1920. As early as January 1920 the synod of the diocese of St. John's resolved:

That this Synod is of the opinion that the Committee appointed by the Provincial Synod of 1919 for the revision of the 'Alternative Form for the Administration of the Holy Communion' as passed in Provincial Synod should publicly invite suggestions on their work of revision before its final presentation to the Provincial Synod.

This resolution, dated 19 January 1920, was printed at the end of the cyclostyled copies of Canon Mason's paper to which reference has already been made, and was, no doubt, very largely influenced by it. Even though by the time that this resolution was passed the 1920 form would not have been published, the bishop of the diocese who was president of the synod would have known what changes were proposed and could have informed the synod of them. The probability is that the diocesan synod was aware of the proposed changes for the 1920 edition and was still unsatisfied by them.

Dissatisfaction with the revised rite of 1920 was echoed even in the diocese of Grahamstown itself. Five priests working in East London, one of the largest towns in the diocese, sent a joint letter to the *Church Chronicle* deploring the invocation of 1919-20. One

[19] *Grahamstown Newsletter*, July 1919.

of the five was Bazeley's brother-in-law. This letter begins with the usual argument based on the rubric on supplementary consecration. Two particular pleas were made: first, that the invocation should be put in the 'normal' place (i.e. before the words of institution), and secondly, that the words 'upon these thy gifts that he may hallow this oblation' should be omitted. Apparently the authors of this letter had not noticed the word 'creatures' or else were not offended at it.

Gould was quick to seize upon the absurdity of describing the place before the narrative of institution as the 'normal' place for the invocation. Quoting Fortescue,[20] he insisted that the consecration prayer must be regarded as a whole and that the order mattered little since sequence of time has no place in man's worship of the eternal God. Bazeley, too, rushed to the defence of the 1920 form. His argument is chiefly a reiteration of his customary interpretation of the Dominical command 'do this'.[21] Bazeley also argued that the Roman rite and 1662 were the only two Western rites without an invocation, that the invocation was 'normal' throughout the rest of Christendom, and that its 'normal' place was after the Institution. This statement obviously requires some qualification. Even 1662 contains a kind of invocation in 'Hear us, O merciful Father . . .', and even the Roman canon is not altogether without any vestige of an invocation. There are also, on the other hand, some non-Roman Western masses in which the invocation is hardly more developed than in the Roman or in 1662.[22] Nevertheless the five priests eventually withdrew 'normal' and substituted 'natural' for it. This was the first skirmish in the great battle of the invocation. It is significant because the dissidents were priests working in the very diocese in which the movement for revision had started, and also because there came to the support of the dissidents the great opponent of the 1919-20 invocation, Dr. John Darragh.

Darragh was a 'man of masterful quality; great driving power; broad humanity; impatient of restraint, yet withal a man who kept his spiritual life at a high level'.[23] He was the first resident

---

[20] *The Mass*, pp. 347–52.
[21] *Church Chronicle*, XVII, p. 231 (cf. *Proposals*, p. 2, and *Theology*, II, p. 161, and also Bishop in *C.Q.R.*, LXVI, p. 387).
[22] See e.g. the Mozarabic mass for Epiphany in Linton, *Twenty-five Consecration Prayers* (S.P.C.K., 1921), pp. 120 ff.
[23] Page, *The Harvest of Good Hope* (S.P.C.K., 1947), p. 37.

Anglican clergyman in the new mining town of Johannesburg and became rector of St. Mary's Church there (now the Johannesburg Cathedral). It was there that his great work was done; but it was there also that he found himself, in the last years of the nineteenth century, at loggerheads with his bishop. He continued, however, to be rector of St. Mary's until, in 1908, 'His strenuous life wore him out; "with a household of almost monastic bareness, he had given away every penny he possessed" and in 1908 "dear Darragh" with his kindly voice and big heart, retired on pension. He settled in Durban. . . .'[24] He would seem to have been, then, a great pastor, a lovable man, and a theologian of some ability (he was the author of *The Resurrection of the Flesh*, S.P.C.K., 1921), but also imperious by nature and a determined, tenacious, and infuriating disputant.

Darragh's entry into the public debate about the invocation came at the point when the five East London priests had made their protest and Dean Hulme of Bloemfontein, in reply, had made his rather weak and muddled attempt to explain it away. Darragh's argument[25] accords very largely with the normal 'Western' approach to the invocation of 1919. He argues that the West, including the Anglican Church, makes the words of Institution consecratory, while the East recites them historically and without ceremonial acts, making the epiclesis the form of consecration. Darragh's reason for classing the Anglican practice so definitely with that of the Roman West rests simply upon the 1662 rubrics attaching the manual acts to the words of Institution. This argument is considered in detail later and is not entirely satisfactory since the 1662 manual acts are patient of quite another interpretation.[26] But they were to become the backbone of all Darragh's arguments against the invocation of 1919. In this, his first public objection to it Darragh asserted that, in the absence of certain knowledge as to the form of words used by our Lord himself in consecrating the first Eucharist, both Eastern and Western forms ought to be pronounced valid. But Gould was, in Darragh's view, trying to impose upon the Province some third form of consecration, neither Eastern nor Western. '. . . in every living liturgy with an Epiclesis it neither precedes nor follows the Form of

---

[24] *Historical Records*, p. 644.
[25] *Church Chronicle*, XVIII, p. 268.
[26] Cf. Gummey, *The Consecration of the Eucharist* (H. F. Ammers Press, 1908), p. 184 n.

Consecration. It is the Form of Consecration.'[27] At this point in the argument the public debate was forcibly stopped by the editor of the *Chronicle* who refused to publish any more letters on the subject for a period of six months. In fact, until the publication of the Natal petition, for which this debate was only a preliminary trial of strength, liturgical affairs remained rather quieter. This preliminary, however, is important because it gives a foretaste of Darragh's stock argument, polished and bolstered up with a good deal of scholarship in the later bouts, which ran like this: East or West—choose one or the other. Either will do for they have agreed to differ. But there must and cannot be any third type.

The year of crisis was 1921. Darragh organized the clergy of the diocese of Natal into petitioning episcopal synod against the invocation of the 1920 form. The synod met in Johannesburg in January 1921. It was the first meeting of the bishops since they had issued the revised form of 1920 almost immediately after the session of provincial synod in November 1919—and it was the first opportunity the dissidents had had for voicing an official protest, since the meeting of the assessors. That Darragh was really responsible for the petition cannot be doubted. On 5 January 1921 he wrote to Frere:

I enclose our petition and the pamphlet in justification of the Petition which the Committee asked me, as a person fairly conversant with liturgical literature, to draw up. The Committee adopted my draft with a few immaterial amendments. Unfortunately the work had to be done against time as a meeting of Episcopal Synod was imminent.[28]

The petition itself, though printed, is undated and bears no printers' name. It has been possible to trace only three copies of it still extant. One is in the minutes of episcopal synod. One is amongst Bishop Frere's papers at Mirfield. The third was found among the books and papers of Canon Gould. All these copies include the explanatory pamphlet referred to by Darragh in his letter to Frere quoted above. The bare text of the petition, without the explanatory notes, was published in the *Church Chronicle*. The date of the framing of the petition is fixed by the reference in Darragh's letter quoted above to the 'meeting of Episcopal Synod' being 'imminent'. Synod met in January 1921, so the work on the petition must have been done in the last weeks of 1920. The copy

[27] *Church Chronicle*, XVIII, p. 340.
[28] Jasper, *Walter Howard Frere*, p. 212.

of the petition inserted into the minutes of the synod is opposite the page dated 10 January 1921.

The petition seems to have been the outcome of official diocesan business. The accompanying explanatory pamphlet, entitled *Considerations, bearing on the Petition to the Episcopal Synod, addressed to the Right Reverend the Lord Bishop of Natal*, is in the form of an open letter to Dr. Baines. It is signed, like the petition itself, by nine clergymen of the diocese, including Darragh himself, W. T. Alston, and Canon M. O. Hodson. After signatures appears a note:

The Committee constituted subsequently to the discussion on this subject at the recent Clergy Conference in Maritzburg, to carry out your Lordship's advice to the Conference.

Presumably the bishop had advised the clergy of the diocese to make their dissatisfaction known by means of a formal petition to the synod. The petition as printed in the *Church Chronicle* has, after the nine signatures, the words 'and the European Clergy with few exceptions'. The same addition has been made in manuscript to the copy of the petition found among Gould's papers.

The petition is short and to the point. It requests the bishops of the Province:

(1) to reconsider the wording of both Invocations . . . in the Alternative Form . . . and especially to clear up the ambiguity of the new Invocation . . .;

(2) to emphasize the tentative and experimental nature of the latest edition of that Form (i.e. 1920);

(3) to bear in mind the desirability of carrying the clergy with them . . .;

(4) and to weigh its effects upon the cohesion of the English Church.

The *Considerations* attached to the petition is a lengthy and closely argued pamphlet dealing almost entirely with the first of these four points alone. The first part of the pamphlet, though it opens with protestations of gratitude for the *Alternative Form*, is really concerned to state the differences between Eastern and Western Christianity in theology of consecration. No evidence is alleged at this point to show that the East and West do, in fact, adopt the rigid and unyielding attitude attributed to them by Darragh, but he does later, in a note appended to the body of the pamphlet, list the evidence for the 'Western use of the words of Institution as the Form of Consecration'. In this note Darragh cites Ambrose, *De Mysteriis* 54, Tertullian, *Adv. Marcion* iv. 40 (doubtful), and *De Sacramentis*. He quotes the last of these from Fortescue's *The Mass* and goes on to say, 'The best brief summing up of the extant evidence for the Eastern Epiclesis is in Father Fortescue's *The Mass*, pp. 402-3'. There follows a long extract from Fortescue beginning, 'The Invocation of the Holy Ghost is not primitive'. Finally Darragh refers to Gelasius I, Optatus, and Isidore, all of whom, he says, 'speak of the Holy Spirit as the agent in consecration' but give 'no indication as to whether the agency of the Holy Spirit was expressed verbally in the Office used'. Frere was later to accuse Darragh of giving a misleading impression by his handling of these three Western writers, for Frere maintained that Darragh gave a false, a deliberately false, evaluation of the evidence for a Western invocation. He had referred to one of two relevant passages from Gelasius, and had ignored the more explicit of the two.[29] He had failed to give the context of Isidore's reference to the Holy Spirit—the passage, that is, in which Isidore deals with the *post-pridie* prayer—a context which probably means that Isidore was, in fact, thinking of a formal invocation of the Holy Spirit.

The whole of this argument on the Western form of consecration, Darragh placed in a brief appendage to the pamphlet. In the body of the pamphlet he assumed that there was a fixed and unquestionable 'Western tradition' to which the South African form adhered. Inevitably Darragh cited the 'third rubric' as the evidence for assigning the *Alternative Form* to the Western tradition. Undoubtedly this rubric was a weak point in the new rite. Frere himself had criticized it, and all that the bishops could say in its defence was:

Play is made with the rubric about supplementary consecration—rather for embarrassment—for clearly it is open for us to claim that the short formula is intended to be covered by the whole Prayer of Consecration. . . . But to claim that a scarcely necessary rubric aimed at an accidental occurrence is to govern the whole scheme of Consecration is monstrous.[30]

Darragh's interpretation of the rubric has, however, a long and

---

[29] Both passages from Gelasius were quoted in Fortescue, *The Mass*, p. 405, so Darragh must have known them. Darragh quotes from Thiel, *Epistolae Romanorum Pontificum* i. 542 (but cf. i. 486 which he does not quote). For Darragh's argument see Jasper, *Walter Howard Frere*, p. 221 n.

[30] Jasper, p. 214.

respectable Anglican ancestry, and it was inconsistent for the
bishops to have added the old 1662 invocation to the form for
supplementary consecration and not to have added the new
invocation which they had especially imported into the rite. If
they were going to argue that the 'third rubric' did not in any way
define the 'form of consecration' but was covered by the whole
of the anaphora, then it would have been sufficient to have used
the form for supplementary consecration provided in 1662. There
was no need to add the 1662 invocation to the form. For it
cannot be argued that the bishops were simply continuing to use
the old form of 1662. In the *Proposed Form* of 1918 they had done
just that, and the 1662 rubric was printed exactly as it had been.
But in 1919, in the first *Alternative Form*, the bishops deliberately
changed the rubric. First, they made it obligatory to reconsecrate
in both kinds. Secondly, they added the first invocation to the
words to be used. It cannot be said that what they did was an
accident, or due to a slip of the proof-reader's eye. They inten-
tionally changed the 1662 form for supplementary consecration,
adding to it the first (the 1662) invocation but not the second, new
one, and in doing so they cut the ground from under their own
feet.

Even more extraordinary than the bishops' inconsistency in this
matter, is the fact that no one seems to have noticed that it was
inconsistent. Of all the people who criticized the new rubric, not
one remarked that it was odd to use the old invocation and yet
not use the new one. Presumably those who criticized the new
form from the Western point of view ignored the inconsistency
because they wished to insist that the *words of Institution alone* were
consecratory, for their argument was equally inconsistent. When
Darragh sought to prove by reference to the 'third rubric' that
the words of Institution were the only essential form of consecration, what he was really proving was that the invocation 'Hear
us, O merciful Father' was similarly indispensable.

Having attempted thus to prove that the *Alternative Form*
belonged firmly in the Western tradition, Darragh next warmed
to his task of dealing with the invocation. 'Our objection is not to
an epiclesis as such, for no known liturgy is without an epiclesis
of some sort . . .' but the 'second epiclesis . . . ignores and
obscures the existing epiclesis in the Prayer of Consecration'. With
complete irrelevance Darragh devotes a part of his pamphlet to

proving that 'invocation of the Holy Spirit' does not mean 'invocation addressed to the Holy Spirit'. As this point was never at issue in the whole of the controversy, it can safely be ignored here. Returning to the main theme of his argument, Darragh points out that the Scottish and American rites have dropped the 'first epiclesis' and that its retention in the South African form is one of the causes of the obscurity and illogicality of the new anaphora. Obviously it would be nonsense to have two formal invocations of the Holy Spirit in the course of one anaphora, but the South African prayer has not done that. If Darragh meant that the prayer has 'two epicleses' in the sense that it has two prayers asking the Father for some special gift, then that is obviously true —but one can see little harm in that. As Darragh's favourite, Fortescue, has said, invocations are to be found 'scattered throughout various liturgies both within and often before the Consecration prayer'.[31]

It is possible to detect, as Lietzmann has detected, a large number of such invocations in the Roman rite. Lietzmann argued that *Te igitur* is 'of the well-known type of those Gallican epicleses in which the petition for the acceptance of the offering is connected with the blessing of it . . . having originally the character of an offertory', that *Hanc igitur* is 'an ancient offertory prayer and has its parallels in Gallican and Mozarabic epicleses'; that *Quam oblationem* is an epiclesis of the type 'in which the blessing of the gifts is sought first, the petition for the outpouring of the Holy Spirit upon the gifts occurring in the second place'; and that *Supplices te* possesses 'the normal termination of the epiclesis . . . in East and West'.[32]

Cirlot has also argued that the early Church probably used the term 'epiclesis' to describe the whole prayer of consecration.[33] If he is correct in this, then the more particular invocations within the prayer may fairly be considered as summing up the intention of the whole prayer at various intervals. Though it may be untidy

---

[31] *The Mass*, p. 404. Fortescue's work is quoted altogether about half a dozen times in Darragh's pamphlet. Darragh later excused his frequent use of Fortescue by saying, 'The local apologists for the "Alternative Form" kept on saying, "Oh, you have only to read Fortescue and you will be convinced that it is all right" (Jasper, *Walter Howard Frere*, p. 225). Frere provoked this statement from Darragh by saying, 'The only original part of Fortescue is his mistakes', a dictum he must have enjoyed since he repeated it (Jasper, pp. 218, 220, and 225).

[32] Lietzmann, *Mass and Lord's Supper* (English translation), pp. 96 ff.

[33] Cirlot, *The Early Eucharist*, p. 194.

to sum up in this way twice in the course of the prayer, it can hardly be condemned as wrong, and it will become apparent later that the South African bishops were, indeed, concerned with the meaning of the whole prayer, and not with any one part of it. The real weakness in the bishops' case at this point was that they had laid so much stress on the great gains in logicality in the new rite and in the anaphora in particular. They claimed, for instance, that the new arrangement made 'the service very much easier of explanation to Confirmation Candidates and others preparing for Communion'.[34] Once they had made such large claims, it was easy to criticize them. In the cause of logic and simplicity they might have been better advised to omit the 'first epiclesis' and concentrate upon the second; but they can hardly be said to be wrong for having left it in. No doubt their chief reason for doing so was to retain as much as possible of 1662 intact.

Darragh's next point in *Considerations* was a classification of eucharistic eucharistic epicleses into three types. The first type is that of the Eastern liturgies. There is nothing to be said about this part of the pamphlet save that it ought to be pointed out that the very passage which Darragh quotes to establish that the Eastern theology of consecration makes the epiclesis the form and moment of consecration, itself considerably modifies the rigidity which he attributes to it:

it will be seen [says Darragh's source] that the Words of the Saviour . . . which the Minister utters as he points to the sacred gifts, and the calling for the Holy Ghost over the gifts, constitute a single, undivided continuous act.[35]

There really is nothing in this quotation to support the division of East and West into two irreconcilable schools of thought each affirming a quite different 'moment of consecration', who have yet somehow 'agreed to differ'. No doubt the East and West do differ. No doubt the East does consider the invocation as the supreme moment of the consecration. But this quotation shows that the Eastern concentration upon the invocation is not one which excludes the narrative of the institution from the 'form of consecration'.

Darragh's second type of invocation is the Western one

[34] *Alternative Form* (1919), p. 2.
[35] *Considerations*, pp. 3 f., quoting Archbishop Macarius of Lithuania, *Dogmatic Theology* (Sacramental Section), pp. 110 f.

'which precedes the consecration'. The South African form, he says, is manifestly different from this type, 'if only by reason of its position'.

The third type of invocation is dismissed in a few words:

In fragments of some Western Liturgies an epiclesis is sometimes found after the Consecration Prayer, appealing to the Father to accept the consecrated elements as a valid Eucharist, and to make it available for the communicants.[36]

The South African invocation, the pamphlet argues, is not of the Eastern type because the 'third rubric' defines the words of Institution as essential for consecration. If the invocation is not itself to be regarded as consecratory, so Darragh's argument runs, then it cannot be of the Eastern type and must, therefore, be one of the Western varieties. But as a Western invocation it is unsatisfactory, because it throws doubt on the validity of the consecration which, in his view, has already been effected by the words of Institution. Darragh argues that to use the word 'creatures' in the two invocations is to suggest that the elements are in the same state after the narrative as before it. Instead of drawing the obvious conclusion—that the bishops might have done this deliberately so as to destroy any possibility of a particular part of the prayer being regarded as alone effective—Darragh continues to hold to the narrowly Roman view on which, indeed, the whole argument of the pamphlet depends. In this view the invocation must be near blasphemy.

To reduce the suggestion of blasphemy and to strengthen the 'Western' interpretation of the prayer, Darragh desired that the first invocation should be amended and rendered less ambiguous. He suggests that 'Hear us . . .' should be recast in the form used in the Scottish Prayer Book of 1637 or in 'Bishop Gore's "A Prayer Book Revised" (pp. 80-1)'.

Strictly speaking, *A Prayer Book Revised* was not 'Bishop Gore's', though the bishop contributed a foreword to it. It was an anonymous work; but a letter found among Canon Gould's papers helps to explain its authorship and the form of invocation used in it.

Dear Mr. Gould,

Thank you very much for sending me the pamphlet on the liturgy. It is most useful and full of good stuff. [This must refer to *Proposals*,

---

[36] But cf. Bishop on '*legitima eucharistia*' in *The Mozarabic and Ambrosian Rites* (Alcuin Club, 1924), p. 50.

for the letter is dated 24 January 1914, and a further paragraph follows on the same subject. Then the letter continues.]

By the way, I am the author of 'A Prayer Book Revised', and I quite agree with what you say about the Epiklesis. The form used was preferred by the Bishop, mainly as not involving too violent a change, and by Brightman, on the ground that it offered a reconciliation between East and West. Brightman takes the view that both Roman and Eastern have a right to their own views, and that we ought not to take sides. But I agree that the Epiklesis had better be in the right place.

If you ever publish a second edition you can say that the Editor of 'A Prayer Book Revised' is quite willing for the Epiklesis to be placed where you have placed it.

The letter is signed by Percy Dearmer. Gould had mentioned *A Prayer Book Revised* in the third of his appendices to *Proposals*; he had given his reasons for preferring not to adopt the kind of invocation that Dearmer had proposed in that book. Dearmer's remarks are a reply to Gould's criticisms. There is no way of telling whether Gould ever used this letter from Dearmer to answer Darragh's argument. Certainly there was never a second edition of *Proposals*.

To return again to the argument of *Considerations*: Darragh's next concern is to show that the South African invocation is based on that of the Scottish rite. In fact the similarity is limited to the words 'thy Holy Spirit upon us and upon these thy gifts', which appear in both rites. Darragh's case that the one depends on the other is a very difficult one to maintain. The South African invocation was really a composite thing, drawn from many sources, and, at least partly, suggested by Frere. But Darragh is determined to see the South African invocation as a derivative of the Scottish; and the Scottish, itself, as a thing of little worth. He devotes three pages of the pamphlet and a long additional note to invective which heaps scorn upon the form, history, and parentage of the Scottish liturgy. There really is no other way to describe this extraordinary and gratuitous polemic. The last paragraph of Darragh's additional note is typical:

Thus we can see that the central and vital part of the Alternative Form is modelled on a Rite, which itself is derived from the moribund Communion Office of a small English Sect, now extinct [the Non-Jurors]. That Office is neither Eastern, nor Western, nor Gallican, nor Laudian, but is frankly, in its strength and its weakness, a characteristic product of the eighteenth century. It is with extreme reluctance that the damaging facts regarding the source of the second Epiclesis in the Alternative Form are here set forth. It is no pleasure to spy out the nakedness of the land. But when certain features of the Scottish Liturgy are offered as sufficient justification for liturgical eccentricities, it is necessary to enquire carefully into its origins.[37]

These derogatory exclamations drew down upon Darragh the wrath of many Scottish clergymen. One of these was A. P. F. Erskine who had earlier condemned the South African anaphora as 'to say the least, a most lamentable bathos, this *false* grafting of East upon West: coming after the *true* grafting of the Scottish Office'. Erskine continued to sympathize with the framers of the Natal petition but he now, nevertheless, strongly resented and attempted to rebut the criticisms that *Considerations* levelled at the Scottish liturgy. The dean of St. Andrew's, with a slower and more stately wrath, also rebuked Darragh for his rudeness.[38]

A comparison of the two invocations, the Scottish and the South African, shows quite plainly that there is no evidence upon which Darragh could base his claim that the South African form was virtually derived from the Scottish. And, in fact, in the face of Scottish anger, Darragh had to withdraw all his calumnies on the Scottish rite, his criticisms of the learning of the Scottish bishops, and his attempt to derive the South African invocation from the Scottish. He contented himself with falling back on the safer, if unoriginal, argument that Erskine had already used, namely that the Scottish liturgy was a true, the South African a false, graft of East upon West. This was a very different thing from his original contention that the South African invocation was bad because the Scottish was worse. The argument from the Scottish rite of 1912 stood revealed as an unsavoury red herring.

A great part of the *Considerations* is devoted to an attempt to use the manual acts of 1662 as a way of interpreting the theology of consecration inherent in the prayer itself. It was Darragh's contention that the Easterns attached no ceremonial to the recital of the words of Institution, whereas the epiclesis was treated ceremonially as the moment of great importance. The last part of this statement is true, of course, and may be admitted without further argument. But Darragh proceeded to claim that the manual acts, taken over into the South African rite of 1919 from the Book of

---

[37] *Considerations*, p. 19.
[38] *Church Chronicle*, XVII, p. 268; XVIII, pp. 39, 94.

1662, mark the words of Institution as the moment of consecration since they attach the only ceremonial laid down by rubric to that part of the prayer. It is obvious that no ceremonial is, by rubric, attached to the invocation of the 1919 rite. The invocation is also, as Darragh contended, very much less definitely worded than the Eastern type. But is it true that the manual acts of 1662, still attached by rubric to the words of Institution in the South African rite, are ceremonial evidence that these words *alone* are to be regarded as consecratory? Even the Eastern liturgies are not completely without 'manual acts' at this point. In the liturgy of St. Chrysostom these acts are performed by the deacon and not by the priest; but the deacon performs the same acts again at the invocation. In St. James the priest is instructed to 'take' at the narrative of the institution, just as he is in the Anglican rites. The Roman rite has only two manual acts at the words of Institution —'taking' and 'signing with the cross'. The only manual act that 1662 shares with the Roman rite (which Darragh used as the norm for the 'Western tradition') is one which it also shares with the Eastern liturgy of St. James. The real ceremonial difference between the East and Rome is that the signing of the elements and the prostration before them comes, in the one case at the invocation, in the other at the words of Institution. Neither prostration nor signing is enjoined by the rubrics of the Book of Common Prayer. The direction to 'take' in the Book of 1662 was probably one of the features which that book inherited from the Scottish Prayer Book of 1637, and it is likely that the ancestry of the Scottish book is to be traced through the Scottish bishops of the time to the Book of Common Order, John Knox, and Calvin, rather than through Laud and the Prayer Book of 1549, to the medieval Latin rites.[39] There is not much ground for the belief that the rubric which directs the priest to 'take' (the only act 1662 shares with the Roman rite) was put into the Book of Common Prayer to enshrine the Roman theory of consecration. Certainly it is true that at least one of the manual acts of 1662, the direction to 'break', was introduced as a result of the representations made by the *puritans* at the Savoy Conference. It is not clear where the direction to 'lay hands upon' came from, but it was not the Roman rite. All in all, it is not easy to prove that the revisers of

[39] Donaldson, *The Making of the Scottish Prayer Book of* 1637 (Edinburgh University Press, 1954), pp. 13, 68 ff.

1661 intended the manual acts to indicate that the words of Institution, and these words *alone*, constituted the 'form of consecration'; to argue from ceremonial, some of which is not fixed by rubric but is simply traditional, seems highly unsatisfactory.

Darragh also argued that the Americans, whose rite contains an invocation after the words of Institution, 'genuflect and elevate at the words of Institution (*vide* Dr. Dearmer's *Art of Public Worship*, p. 105 n.) shewing that they regard the Consecration as already effected . . .'.[40] Dearmer's note, in fact, reads, 'It is quite surprising, for instance, in America, to find priests who genuflect and elevate at the Words of Institution, as if there were no other theory of Consecration than the Roman, and the plain words of the American *anaphora* had no meaning whatever'. Dr. Gummey's *Consecration of the Eucharist*, already several times referred to, is an American work devoted to showing that the invocation is the 'form of consecration' in the American rite, so it is clear that there are some Americans, at least, who do not fall within Darragh's judgement that 'in practice . . . they take the Invocation . . . in something of a Gallican sense'.

Two other points from the *Considerations* need to be particularly noted. First Darragh argued that the timelessness of eternity is no excuse for illogicality in the arrangement of a rite. There were those who argued that consecration was a timeless act and that the order of the parts of the anaphora was not important. Darragh rightly retorted that, if that were so, and the order of the parts did not matter, 'what becomes of the talk of "dislocation" in our Prayer Book Service, and the claim that revision is for the purpose of remedying that dislocation?'[41] But Darragh entirely ignores the fact that the placing of the invocation after the words of Institution has a logic of its own, since the place of the invocation is probably fixed by the idea of Pentecost at the end of the anamnesis, though Pentecost is not mentioned in the South African anaphora. The other point to be noted is that Darragh argues that the Gallican anaphoras afford no precedent for the South African rite, since they are variable. Obviously, Darragh argues, what is an essential part of the prayer could not be virtually omitted on one day and be included on another. This argument has a convincing ring, and no doubt it carried convic-

[40] *Considerations*, p. 12.
[41] *Considerations*, p. 12, cf. *Proposed Form* (1918), p. 3.

tion to many who were doubtful about the revised rite. Its validity depends entirely, however, upon the view Darragh takes of the history of the Gallican masses. It is true that some of the later non-Roman Western masses have invocations so vague as sometimes hardly to be invocations at all, but one might well prefer to hold, with W. C. Bishop, 'that the invocation [in these cases] has been whittled away and finally discarded under the influence of a doctrinal prepossession'.[42]

For a convenient summary of the argument of the pamphlet it may be as well to give a series of quotations from Darragh's own summing-up.

To sum up—if it is desired to discard the Western method of consecration and adopt the Eastern usage, let us have the real thing. Sweep away from the Words of Institution the traditional ceremonial [i.e. the manual acts] of the West, and let them be recited historically, as they are in Eastern Liturgies, and then let the Consecration follow, using the genuine Epiclesis of the East in its ancient Form. If we are not prepared to do that, let us cease to talk of following the Eastern Tradition. . . .

Again if we wish to add to our existing epiclesis—'Hear us, O merciful Father'—a post-consecration epiclesis after the manner of some Gallican Masses, a genuine one would surely be better than a modern imitation. . . . But we would venture to submit . . . that the revival amongst us of features taken from Liturgies long extinct, should be done with extreme caution. . . .

The Home Church has had the Revision of the Prayer Book in hand for a dozen years, with the advantage of a scholarship to which we in this Province cannot pretend, including that of the eminent liturgiologists Brightman, Frere and W. C. Bishop. It is surely worthy of note that they have left the Consecration Prayer untouched, except that the Prayer of Oblation is to be used immediately after it. . . .

It is interesting to note that when Bishop heard what Darragh had said about him he wrote to Gould:

My most fixed idea is that the invocation should come *after* the narrative of the institution, and if the idea has gone forth that I am in favour of the invocation coming *before* the institution, I should be obliged to you to contradict it as widely as possible.[43]

Frere's view as to the position of the invocation agreed, of course, with that of Bishop, and he made it clear to Darragh that it did so.[44] Brightman, alone, might be thought to be more sympathetic

---

[42] Bishop in *C.Q.R.*, LXVI, p. 395.
[43] Gould quoting a private letter from Bishop in *Church Chronicle*, XVIII, p. 215.
[44] Jasper, *Walter Howard Frere*, p. 220.

to Darragh's argument. When Bishop Nash wrote to solicit Frere's help against Darragh's criticisms of the 1920 form he said, 'Darragh has written to F. E. Brightman and got him to curse us. But the same F. E. B. said to me—for I sent him a copy—"It's all right". But he seems to have been impressed by the Supplementary Consecration argument.'[45] Unfortunately, neither Brightman's 'curse' nor his earlier, rather grudging approval, has survived. But it is clear that his views did later harden against such an invocation—and perhaps Darragh's argument was partly responsible, as Nash suggested—for by 1927 Brightman was writing:

there is no real contrast between prayer [i.e. invocation] and the recital [of the narrative of institution] since the recital is a part of a continuous prayer and is itself explicitly addressed to the Eternal Father. . . . And indeed the recital might be said to represent a higher type of prayer than a petition for the coming of the Holy Ghost, since it simply, so to speak, lays the situation before God for Him to do what He will.[46]

In the same article Brightman described the invocation of the proposed English rite of 1927 as being by its position 'a gratuitous departure from our tradition'.

This Invocation of 1549 . . . is Western in its whole substance . . . the order of 1549 is, to say the least of it, wholly defensible, and gives us all we need desire without any departure from Western precedent.

Brightman makes no reference to the invocation of the South African rite in this particular article, and we have no direct means of knowing what his reaction to it was, in so many words, but these extracts make it clear that his general attitude was no longer that the invocation should come before the words of Institution because 'we ought not to take sides', but because we ought very definitely to take the 'Western' side. Brightman did, in the course of the article quoted above, refer to the South African anaphora in order to criticize its inclusion of the Lord's prayer under the general heading of THE CONSECRATION. Otherwise he did not mention it; no doubt because by that time the South African invocation had been emasculated and there was no need for comment.

[45] Jasper, p. 215.
[46] Brightman in a pamphlet entitled *The Alternative Canon* (Oxford University Press, 1927), p. 5; also published in *C.Q.R.* (July 1927), CIV, pp. 219 ff., under the title 'The New Prayer Book Examined'.

To return to Darragh's *Considerations*: it is clear that his argument depends upon two fundamental assumptions: first, that both Eastern and Western theories of consecration are 'of ecumenical allowance' and 'are catholic', but that there is no other possible 'catholic' theory; and secondly that the manual acts and the 'third rubric' prove that the South African rite embodies the 'Western' theory. The bishops who had framed the rite did not want to specify any 'moment of consecration'. Nash, a member of the liturgical committee, wrote to Frere in these terms about the notorious rubric: 'Clearly it is open for us to claim that the short formula allowed is intended to be covered by the whole prayer of consecration.'[47] The bishops as a whole confirmed this later, saying:

they [the bishops] hold to the primitive view . . . that when thanksgiving has been offered in prayerful trust that God's Power will accomplish his purpose, we then can securely believe in the Presence of Our Lord in the Eucharist, without debating the exact moment when the Presence was granted. This applies to the Canon equally in the B.C.P. and in the Alternative Form. We are not tied to the belief that in the B.C.P. the narrative is the moment, any more than that in the Alternative Form the Epiclesis is the moment.[48]

This surely suggests that the revisers intended the whole prayer, and not any specific part of it, to be consecratory. There was a fundamental disagreement between them and Darragh as to what views were 'of ecumenical allowance'. Darragh was not prepared to countenance any view except the rigid Eastern or rigid Western. The bishops were caught in the tangle of their own making. They had been careless in the framing of the rubric on supplementary consecration. That they failed to include the new invocation in the form to be used, particularly when they were at pains to include, quite deliberately and definitely, the old invocation from 1662, must seem an inexplicable, and almost incredible, piece of muddle and folly. To be consistent they ought really to have specified that the whole prayer was to be used again or at least the greater part of it. The omission of the new invocation, when the old was included in the form, suggested that the new invocation was not regarded as at all consecratory.

It appears from the minutes that when episcopal synod met on

[47] Jasper, *Walter Howard Frere*, p. 214.
[48] Report of Liturgical Committee to Episcopal Synod, Nov. 1921.

10 January 1921, Phelps reported that the liturgical committee had not met since the last session of the synod in October and November 1919, when the assessors' suggestions had been considered. Apparently, episcopal synod received the Natal petition, for a copy was inserted in the minutes. The liturgical committee was reappointed to consider the whole question of the revised form, and to report back to the synod on any further alterations it thought desirable to make 'before the Form is finally passed by the next Provincial Synod'. The phrase quoted directly from the resolution of the synod is deceptive. If no changes had been made, and if provincial synod had agreed to pass the 1919-20 form again, that would have given it final effect. But as the liturgical committee materially altered the form of 1920, it needed to be passed twice more, by consecutive sessions of provincial synod. No doubt the language of the resolution reflected the desire of the bishops to have the matter finally settled with as little further unrest as possible.

Episcopal synod issued an official report of its proceedings in which this resolution was given in full. The announcement that the bishops had returned the *Alternative Form* to the liturgical committee did nothing to quieten the alarm felt in a great many parts of the country at the course revision was taking. The Natal petition provoked a great deal of argument and discussion—most of it aired in the columns of the *Chronicle*. In particular the signatories of the petition found themselves involved in two serious and important controversies by correspondence.

Bishop Nash, member of Frere's community and coadjutor bishop of Cape Town, was one of the leading figures in the liturgical committee. Early in 1921 he emerged as the great champion of the 1919 rite. Soon after the close of the 1921 session of episcopal synod he wrote to Frere asking for his assistance in controverting Darragh. Darragh also wrote two letters to Frere. All these letters are printed in full in R. C. D. Jasper's *Walter Howard Frere* and need not be dealt with in detail here.[49] There is no doubt where Frere's sympathies lay. He was indignant about some of Darragh's arguments, and the lameness of Darragh's reply to Frere's criticisms shows who had really won the argument. Darragh tried desperately to maintain that the East and West had agreed to differ and that Rome allows 'both methods' (of con-

[49] pp. 212 ff.

secration) within her jurisdiction. But this is not really true. Rome allows both rites; but attaches certain conditions to the use of the Eastern rite. In the Uniat missals the words of institution are specifically called the words of consecration, and the elevation is prescribed.[50] The rite is allowed, but not the form of consecration, though it is true that the invocation is permitted to follow the words of institution without any suggestion of blasphemy.

Darragh appears, in fact, to have been wrong on both counts. Neither the East nor the West has quite such a rigid form of consecration as Darragh supposed: Rome can allow invocation to follow the dominical words; the East can speak of the two together forming a continuous whole. Nor is it true that there has been an agreement to differ, with each allowing the narrow and rigid form of the other as a kind of second-best. In fact any 'agreement to differ' is only made possible by the fact that neither Rome nor the East possesses so rigid a form of consecration as Darragh desired to attribute to them.

Darragh had failed, too, to make the best of his material. He failed to quote or refer to some of the obvious authorities which support the Western view. Frere was impatient and condescending, and Darragh lost his temper. The correspondence tended to degenerate into an exchange of personal remarks.

The other correspondence was more public. Again it was Nash who put the bishops' point of view. He replied to the Natal petition in a letter sent to the *Church Chronicle*, in which he said:

In general I should think that the position of the petitioners as against the Form proposed by the Bishops and so far accepted by the Province is this: They hold the extreme theory which attaches consecration to this or that special form of words.[51]

Aquinas, he said, had laid down the form of consecration as the words used in the Latin mass—not the same words or the same language as used in 1662—and Rome will allow no other form. The bishops desired to go back to the idea of the whole offering of the priest and people which wins a blessing, and especially to the whole prayer of consecration, not these words or those. Nash goes on to point out the difficulties inherent in attempting to prove the Western theology of consecration from the text or

---

[50] Frere, *The Anaphora*, p. 194. Frere quotes the rubrics and gives a confusing reference to Brightman where the rubrics do not appear.
[51] XVIII, p. 71.

ceremonial of the Roman rite. Then followed a spirited, but not entirely convincing, defence of the weakest point in the bishops' case, the 'third rubric'.

Canon Morris Hodson, one of the signatories, replied for the petitioners, maintaining that they did not necessarily hold to any extreme theory attaching consecration to any particular form, but arguing that theology of consecration is not a matter to be decided by the opinion of scholars, but by the belief of the whole Church, or at least of a Patriarchate. The South African rite possessed a form of consecration sanctioned by no Catholic consent or usage.

Gould, in turn, answered Hodson, pointing out that no hostile critic of the South African rite had been able to cite any decree of Eastern or Western Christendom, fixing a 'moment of consecration'. Still less had anyone cited any decree which could serve as evidence that Rome and the East had agreed to differ.

Nash also returned answer to Hodson. He had apparently been testing Eastern opinion, and for the first time he admitted that the rubric on supplementary consecration was not altogether satisfactory.

Mr. Borough, chaplain at our Crimean Church in Constantinople, writes that Professor Komnenos (of the Theological College at Halki) came to see him. He had studied the South African form of consecration and he pronounced it quite satisfactory. I had specially called attention to the rubric for additional consecration, and he said very decidedly that the Epiklesis must be repeated in such cases. This Dr Frere, the 'Church Times', and others have urged. The matter of manual acts and reverences he did not appear to regard as important.[52]

In the meantime the bishops had received yet another petition —this time from some of the clergy of the diocese of Cape Town. Though less strongly worded than the appeal from Natal, the new petition was obviously intended to make the same point. The Cape Town petition pleaded that 'to annul or subordinate the 1662 Epiklesis, while retaining it in connection with the words of Institution, is a serious departure from the English Tradition'.[53] The petition asked that the new invocation should be made 'clearer and more definite and, if intended to consecrate, this should be unmistakably expressed'. It also said that the new invocation would be better placed before the words of Institution.

[52] *Church Chronicle*, xviii, p. 247; but cf. *Russian Observations on the American Prayer Book* (Alcuin Club), pp. 2, 35.
[53] *Church Chronicle*, xviii, p. 199.

The leader of the new group of petitioners would seem to have been the Rev. Fr. H. P. Bull of the Society of St. John the Evangelist (Cowley Fathers), since it was he who defended and explained it publicly. Fr. Bull had worked in the diocese of Cape Town earlier in his ministry, but he was in 1921 Superior-General of the community. According to the *Cowley Evangelist* (official periodical of the S.S.J.E.), Bull arrived in Cape Town in the Holy Week of 1921, intending originally to stay for three weeks. The illness of one of the members of the community, however, led Fr. Bull to stay on for some time, long enough, in fact, to attend a session of the Cape Town diocesan synod. The *Cowley Evangelist* does not mention the *Alternative Form*, but Bull's longer stay in Cape Town gave him the opportunity to become familiar with the rite, and attendance at the synod allowed him to make contact with those dissatisfied with it. No doubt his fortuitous stay in Cape Town accounted for the apparent surprise caused by the presentation of the petition. It is otherwise hard to explain why the petition should have been drawn up so suddenly and unexpectedly after such a long interval. There was a gap of fully twelve months and more between the publication of the revised rite of 1920 and the Cape Town petition.

Bull's arguments, in his covering letter to the petition, agree with Darragh's in the main. They add nothing to the weight of the objections put forward in *Considerations*; but the existence of the petition was a sign of the growth of the dissatisfaction with the revised rite and of the fact that it was now widespread. Gould wrote of the petitions:

Two of the most justly loved and honoured priests in South Africa Mr. Darragh and Father Bull . . . head the protests against the Alternative Form. Arguments that have been discussed in Natal for twelve months suddenly emerge from Cape Town, and are heard from the Transvaal.[54]

The distant mutterings from the Transvaal, heard by Gould, were an expression of the uneasiness of some of the clergy in the diocese of Pretoria. In June 1921 a pamphlet was published in that diocese entitled *The Liturgy or Order for the Celebration of Holy Communion*. The front cover bore the printed note, 'Proof copy for further consideration and report'. From the way in which the rite itself is set out in the pamphlet, it is clear that it is meant not

[54] *Church Chronicle*, XVIII, p. 215.

for use in celebrating the eucharist—at any rate at the stage reached at the time of the pamphlet—but for study and further revision. Some prayers are not printed in full but are indicated simply by the first and last words; references, printed in heavier type than the rest of the text, have been inserted into the draft to refer the reader to explanatory notes printed at the end of the pamphlet. Only three copies of this draft liturgy can now be traced. One is in the Central Church Record Library; another is in the South African Public Library; the third was among the papers of the late Canon Gould. The outline of the liturgy is:

Either the Litany or the Lord's Prayer and Collect for Purity
Ninefold *Kyries*
Gloria in Excelsis (revised translation)
Collect, Epistle, and Gospel
Sermon and Dismissal of Catechumens
Creed (revised translation)
Offertory
Prayer for the Church (with some additions and alterations)
Sursum Corda, Preface, and *Sanctus*
Consecration Prayer
Lord's Prayer
Pax, Agnus, and Priest's communion
Confession, Absolution, and Comfortable Words
Either Prayer of Humble Access or 'Lord, I am not worthy etc.'
Communion of the People
Either proper Post-Communion or 1662 Prayer of Thanksgiving
Blessing

The anaphora is interesting. It is headed 'Consecration' and begins with the salutation and the *Sursum corda*, and then proceeds as in 1662 as far as '. . . Everlasting God', though Frere's proposed repunctuation of the Preface has been more or less adopted. The *Sanctus* is in its full form—*Sanctus, Hosanna, Benedictus, Hosanna*—and then the prayer continues, 'holy indeed and Blessed indeed art Thou, O Almighty God, our heavenly Father . . .'. The rest of the prayer is much as it was in the 1919 rite, but the invocation runs, 'We . . . entreat thee that thy Holy Spirit may descend upon us and upon this oblation of the Body and Blood of thy Son Jesus Christ our Lord'. The rubric providing for supplementary consecration says that the form is to be 'as Alternative Form, latest edition, 1920', that is to say, 'Hear us, O merciful Father . . . in remembrance of me.'

Since the pamphlet is dated from Johannesburg, it is reasonable to suppose that it was framed in the diocese in which that city then lay, the diocese of Pretoria. A comparison of the draft liturgy with the reports of the subcommittee of the bishop of Pretoria's senate confirms this supposition. Pages 6-15 of the subcommittee's Report to the Lord Bishop of Pretoria, dated 31 January 1919, deal with 'The Liturgy or Order for Celebration of Holy Communion'—the wording is the same as the title of the draft rite. The general principles 'approved by the Committee' are:

Gloria in Excelsis to be at the beginning—N.B. This hymn requires amendment.
The Prayer for the Church to remain as at present.
The Sermon and Notices to precede the Creed (i.e. before the dismissal of the Catechumens).
The Consecration Prayer to be followed by: Prayer of Oblation. Lord's Prayer (with introduction and doxology). The Communion of the Priest. The Communion Devotions en bloc. Communion of the People. Post Communion or Thanksgiving. Blessing.

Other suggestions from the report include substituting the *Kyries* for the Decalogue, adding the *Benedictus* to the *Sanctus*, and the use of the *Agnus Dei*. The recommendations regarding the consecration prayer were:

Connecting link. Read 'Holy indeed and Blessed indeed art Thou, O Almighty God, our Heavenly Father . . .'.
'to take our nature upon him'—approved.
His ONE oblation. Stet. (Not OWN as Scottish.)
The link for the Prayer of Oblation, 'Wherefore'—approved.
The best way of [providing a reference in the anaphora to the Holy Spirit] appears to be that suggested by Frere.

The agreements between this report and the draft rite are so marked that there must have been a direct dependence of the one upon the other. The draft rite is the continuation of the work done in the report. Since the report was intended for the bishop of Pretoria, and since the rite depends upon it, the rite was probably intended for him too.[55] What happened to it after that is a matter for conjecture. Some copies of the rite appear to have been circulated outside the diocese of Pretoria. But no copy of the

---

[55] By this time Furse, the bishop to whom the report had been made, had been translated to St. Albans. The new bishop of Pretoria was Neville Talbot.

pamphlet has been preserved among the papers of the liturgical committee or of episcopal synod.

It is curious that the draft liturgy should have been published so late. The various parts of the Pretoria report are dated between 13 November 1918 and 13 February 1919. They are all earlier, that is to say, than the session of episcopal synod that issued the *Alternative Form* of 1919. The draft liturgy is dated 24 June 1921, more than two years after the Pretoria committee made its report. It seems extraordinary that the committee, having gone to such great pains to produce so voluminous a report (it runs to nearly sixty pages of single-spaced foolscap typewriting) should have neglected to do anything further for two whole years, while the progress of revision made their work out of date and less valuable. Still more extraordinary is the fact that, after such a long period of neglect, it should have been thought worth while to publish a printed form of a rite embodying the suggestions of the report.

The explanation of this curious delay is to be found in Gould's remark on the growth of opposition to the 1919 form quoted above. The work of the Pretoria committee was completed too late for it to have much effect upon the *Alternative Form* of 1919/20. Once the bishops had issued their revised rite and it had been approved by provincial synod in 1919, there was no further point in the Pretoria committee proceeding with an independent revision of their own. But as soon as the objections to the invocation of 1919 had been made public and it was clear that there was a substantial body of opinion which did not favour the *Alternative Form*, the Pretoria committee seized the opportunity to revive their own suggestions and published them in the form of a draft rite. In most respects the rite was modelled even more closely upon Frere's suggestions of 1918 than the official *Alternative Form* of 1919 had been. But by 1921 Frere was discredited in one particular among those who preferred a more 'Western' form of consecration. In the previous year, for instance, Darragh had written:

Father Frere is entirely within a scholar's rights in preferring an Epiklesis to the Western Form. Both are of ecumenical allowance. But in every living liturgy with an Epiklesis, it neither precedes nor follows the Form of Consecration. It is the Form of Consecration.[56]

Frere was plainly regarded, then, as one who 'preferred the

[56] *Church Chronicle*, XVII, p. 340.

Epiklesis'. Ridout, the secretary of the Pretoria committee, wrote a letter to the *Church Chronicle* in which he said:

. . . in regard to the clause 'hallow this oblation'. This clause was suggested by Dr. Frere in July 1918 in his 'Rough Notes on the Proposed Form of the South African Liturgy'. But clearly the words are not intended to be consecratory. His clause runs 'this oblation of the Body and Blood of thy Son'. I was one of a committee of this Diocese, appointed by Bishop Furse, who endorsed that clause, also with no intention that it be regarded as consecratory. Everyone of that committee whom I have been able to consult, now desires their deletion. And the present Bishop of Pretoria has given permission for this Diocese to use the latest Alternative Form with the omission of this clause and of the words 'and creatures of thine own'.[57]

Ridout's letter was written at about the same time as the draft liturgy was published. The invocation of the draft runs: '. . . we entreat thee that thy Holy Spirit may descend upon us and upon this oblation of the Body and Blood of thy Son Jesus Christ our Lord.' Frere's original suggestion had been: 'May thy Holy Spirit descend upon these offerings and hallow this oblation of the Body and Blood of thy Son Jesus Christ our Lord.'

What the Pretoria committee had done was to take Frere's suggestion and omit from it the one phrase that had appeared in the *Alternative Form*, 'hallow this oblation'. The other differences between the two forms, Frere's and the committee's, are slight and are to be explained by the fact that the committee desired that the prayer for the illapse of the Spirit should not in any way specify any activity as a result of the illapse. The other phrase in the South African anaphora directly derived from Frere, 'We offer here unto thy Divine Majesty these sacred gifts and creatures of thine own, this holy bread of eternal life, this cup of everlasting salvation', was also omitted.

The authors of the draft rite were uneasy about Frere's form of the invocation, and particularly about those parts of it which had been used in the *Alternative Form*, and this in spite of the fact that almost all Frere's other suggestions contained in his memorandum of 1918 had been incorporated into the Pretoria proposal. The long-delayed publication of the committee's rite was the result of the public and heated controversy over the South African invocation.

[57] *Church Chronicle*, xviii, p. 268.

Episcopal synod met, for the second time that year, on 7 November 1921. Liturgical matters were considered on 15 November and Phelps presented a report from the liturgical committee. The report stated that, while many people had expressed their gratitude for the *Alternative Form*, 'a widely signed memorial makes it clear that if the phrases "these sacred gifts and creatures of thine own" and "that he may hallow this oblation" were removed . . . the Alternative Form would be generally accepted . . .'.

Synod resolved to excise the phrases referred to, and there can be no doubt that, from a practical point of view at least, they were well advised to do so. The diocese of St. John's had passed a resolution in synod asking the bishops to reconsider the rite of 1919. The clergy of the diocese of Bloemfontein had been given permission by their vicar-general to omit the offensive phrases. The bishop of Pretoria had adopted the same course, and the liturgical subcommittee of his senate had even contemplated an independent revision. The great body of the clergy of the diocese of Natal had petitioned against the invocation, and the clergy of Cape Town had joined them in their protest. Even in Grahamstown, the very home of revision, there were protests and dissatisfaction. Only the missionary dioceses of Zululand and Lebombo, Southern Rhodesia, in the far north, the remote island diocese of St. Helena, and the two small rural dioceses of George and Kimberley, had made no public protest.

But synod resolved at the same time 'to emphasize' the very important statement about the form of consecration which has already been referred to:

they hold to the primitive view . . . that, when thanksgiving has been offered in prayerful trust that God's power will accomplish His purpose, we then can securely believe in the Presence of Our Lord in the Eucharist, without debating the exact moment when the Presence was granted. This applies to the Canon equally in the B.C.P. and in the Alternative Form. We are not tied to the belief that in the B.C.P. the narrative is the moment, any more than that in the Alternative Form the Epiclesis is the moment.

To this they added the statement that

the excision . . . still leaves the memorial of the Holy Ghost in its normal position in the orderly sequence of the Canon, and thus the Canon is in close agreement with the earliest form of the Liturgy.[58]

[58] *Church Chronicle*, XVIII, p. 396.

Thus the amendment to the 1919 form first suggested by Hulme was adopted, and the so-called Bloemfontein use became the use of the Province so far as the invocation was concerned. The notorious 'third rubric' was altered to read, as in the present South African rite, 'either in both kinds, repeating the words of the Consecration Prayer beginning at "Hear us, O Merciful Father", and ending at "heavenly benediction"; or in either kind according to the form given for this purpose in the Book of Common Prayer'.

The liturgical committee also recommended that the advice of the 'Lambeth' Committee on Liturgical Matters should be sought on a number of points. Episcopal synod apparently approved this recommendation, but nothing seems to have been done to implement the suggestion, at least for the time being.

Clearly the 'Western' school had gained a notable concession.

Some of us had hoped that any controversy between the so-called Eastern and Western theories of consecration could have been avoided. But it was not to be. The Natal clergy, headed by the late Dr. Darragh, made the latent opposition vocal in a petition addressed to the Episcopal Synod . . . and two private revisions were printed for circulation, one in Johannesburg, and the other in Natal. With thankfulness one records that all this activity lead [sc. led] not to barren controversy but to concord. The different parties agreed to the compromise already mentioned, by which the Episcopal Synod of 1921 removed the disturbing words from the consecration prayer.[59]

This is Gould's account of what happened, written two years after the controversy had ended. He represented the result as a compromise, and a compromise it was in that the invocation was retained, but in a vaguer and reduced form. The bishops' firm and unequivocal statement about the form and moment of consecration means, however, that the rationale of consecration had not been compromised by the change. The whole section of the rite from *Sursum corda* onwards was labelled CONSECRATION— there was no 'moment' specially emphasized. In every other respect, the rite of 1922 must have seemed a triumph for the Westernizing party. The bishops' statement considerably modified the completeness of that triumph; and the anamnesis and invocation were, in fact, retained. Yet the report of the episcopal synod from which the bishops' statement has been quoted is comparatively obscure.

[59] Gould in *Church Chronicle*, XXI, p. 756.

The Western group might be excused for thinking that they had won their case.

The excision of the offending phrases was the only change made in the edition of 1922, and the anaphora of that edition is identical with the final form. Some unimportant amendments had yet to be made to the rest of the rite, but otherwise, apart from the experiments to be discussed in the next chapter, the revision of the rite was done.

There is a strong and persistent tradition in the Province that Bazeley and Gould were almost entirely responsible for the form which the revised eucharistic rite has taken. The story as it has been told here shows that that tradition requires considerable modification. If Bazeley and Gould had had their way the rite might have been very different and, perhaps, rather better. It is true that they both defended the South African liturgy faithfully and loyally. They influenced the theology of consecration which underlies the revision. Phelps, as chairman of the liturgical committee, was probably often guided by their advice and assistance. There is certainly evidence to prove that there was a close and continuing association between the three men throughout the course of revision. But there is no evidence to show that either Bazeley or Gould played much direct part in the shaping of the details of the rite after 1919.

CHAPTER SIX

THE FINAL FORM

THE REST of the story is straightforward and simple. Episcopal synod made the significant decision to omit the 'disturbing' phrases from the invocation on 15 November 1921. Four days later a new draft liturgy was published in Durban. A covering letter attached to the draft described it as the work of the 'Natal Committee'. This must have been the same committee as had been 'constituted subsequently to the discussion . . . at the recent Clergy Conference' and had commissioned Darragh to draw up the Natal petition. The draft rite was apparently sent out to a number of people, though few copies of it now exist. The covering letter, signed by Darragh, is addressed 'To the Clergy of the Province of South Africa and extra-Provincial Students of Liturgiology'. It begins by stating that the intention of the Natal committee was to ask for criticisms and suggestions before the draft was submitted to the bishops. The liturgy itself, like Darragh's covering letter, has an imposing title: 'An Alternative Liturgy or Order for the Celebration of the Holy Eucharist and Administration of the Holy Communion, Set forth by authority for use in the Church of the Province of South Africa. 192—.' The blank in the date indicates that the latter part of the title reflects the hopes of those who framed the rite, rather than its factual status. Moreover, a note printed in brackets at the top of the cover-page reads:

Draft of suggested amendments to be presented to the Committee of Bishops which has been appointed to reconsider the Alternative Form of 1920. The Amendments are incorporated in the text to facilitate a decision on their suitability and appropriateness.

The liturgy was quite obviously, then, without official standing in the Province. It was strictly a revision of the 1919/20 *Alternative Form* and not a fresh adaptation of the 1662 Book; yet it was a drastic revision of the *Alternative Form* in many ways.

The order of the proposed rite was:

Invocation of the Trinity
Psalm xliii (with the antiphon arranged as versicle and response)

Either the penitential section from the B.C.P. or a short confession
based on the Sarum and Roman models but without invocation of
saints

Lord's Prayer

Prayer from the Sarum rite, 'Take away from us all our iniquities . . .'

Collect for Purity (really a reduplication of the preceding prayer)

Decalogue, ninefold *Kyries*, or Summary of the Law (from Deut. vi. 5
and Lev. xix. 8)

Collect, epistle, and gospel

Creed

Offertory Prayer (similar to prayer in present South African rite)

Prayer for the Church (greatly altered)

Sursum corda, Preface, *Sanctus*, and *Benedictus*

Consecration Prayer (revised)

Agnus

Prayer of Humble Access or 'Lord, I am not worthy etc.'

Communion

Prayer of Thanksgiving

Gloria in Excelsis

Versicle and response, 'Let us depart in peace etc.'

Blessing

The consecration prayer of this rite is specifically stated by
rubric to begin immediately after the *Benedictus*. The *Sanctus* is in
its 1662 form, ending 'Glory be to Thee, O Lord Most High', and
is followed by the *Benedictus* and *Hosanna*. Since the Natal
committee obviously thought of the *Sanctus* and *Benedictus* as
quite distinct from the consecration prayer it is not surprising to
find that the opening words of the prayer do not echo the closing
words of the *Benedictus*. Instead the prayer starts with the phrase
used in the 1919 form, 'All Glory and Thanksgiving be to
Thee . . .'. The first part of the Natal prayer is exactly as the
prayer is printed in 1662, except that it has the phrase 'to take our
nature upon Him', and the invocation is amended to read:

Hear us, O merciful Father, and graciously send down Thy Holy Spirit
upon these Thy creatures, that He may make this bread the precious
Body, and this wine the precious Blood, of Thy Son, our Saviour
Jesus Christ, according to His holy institution—Who in the same
night. . . .

This invocation was taken, with very few changes, from the
liturgy of St. John Chrysostom. The whole part of the prayer
corresponding to the 1662 consecration prayer is printed in capital

letters and concludes with an *Amen*. Then follows the rest of the anaphora of the 1919 form, printed as a separate prayer and in ordinary type. The second invocation was changed to read:

and we humbly beseech Thee to pour Thy Holy Spirit upon us and upon these Sacred Mysteries of Christ's Body and Blood, to the intent that we may fruitfully receive the same and be fulfilled with Thy grace and heavenly benediction.

Then *Amen* is said again before the rest of the prayer is recited.

The implications of this rearrangement of the consecration prayer are important, especially when they are compared with the argument Darragh had put forward in *Considerations*. There is obviously a very different approach to the theology of consecration. Since Darragh signed the covering letter which went out with the draft rite, it is convenient to regard him as the author of the rite. No doubt, officially, both *Considerations* and the draft liturgy were the work of the Natal committee; but Darragh appears to have been at least the moving spirit behind both pamphlets. The important thing, however, is not the authorship so much as the marked change in attitude. The committee (which probably means Darragh) had changed its mind, for the Natal draft rite does not appear to regard the words of Institution as *alone* consecratory. The whole of the prayer from 'All Glory' to the end of the narrative of Institution is printed in capital letters. The rubric directing the form for supplementary consecration is identical with that of the *Alternative Form* of 1919, prescribing the use of the whole prayer from 'Hear us, O merciful Father' to 'Do this as oft as ye shall drink it in remembrance of me'. Remembering the importance which Darragh had attached to the rubric in the 1919 form we can hardly doubt that he intended it to define the 'form of consecration'. It is, therefore, of the highest importance to note that this form of consecration included the invocation 'Hear us, O merciful Father', in its new shape. It is, in wording though not position, an invocation of the Greek type, so that the form of consecration in the Natal rite is not the words of Institution alone, but these words together with the amended invocation. The only difference between the Natal rite and the 1919 form is the position of the invocation and the fact that the Natal invocation is itself far more precisely worded and far more 'Eastern'.

It is worth noting that the Natal rite does not solve the time-sequence problem. In altering the wording of the 1662 invocation on a Greek model, it has removed from the invocation any sense of futurity and makes it a prayer for present action. Cranmer's 1549 invocation avoided that implication by making a clear link between the action of the Holy Spirit and the words of Institution, 'With thy Holy Spirit and Word vouchsafe to bless and sanctify these thy gifts . . .'. Darragh's criticism of the invocation of 1919/20 might be alleged in return against the Natal rite. In the latter there is a very strongly worded invocation which, taken at its face value, seems to speak of consecration being effected at the moment of its recitation. This invocation is then followed by the words of Institution. Because the Natal committee used a Greek model rather than 1549, all they have managed to suggest is that consecration is already effected before the recitation of the narrative is even begun. If the words 'that He may make . . .' had been used at any other point in the prayer by the official revisers of the Province, they would certainly have been interpreted in this absolute sense by Darragh and his supporters.

The other point of interest is the *Amen* after the second invocation—now a prayer for fruitful reception. Compare with this, Darragh's remarks about the South African invocation:

The epiclesis in the . . . Alternative Form is an excellent preparation for consecration, but no form of Consecration, known to East or West, follows. No pause is made to acknowledge a great act of God the Holy Ghost. The service goes on without the faintest sign by word or act, that Our Lord has vouchsafed His Sacramental Presence—not so much as an *Amen*.[1]

To have introduced the *Amen* after the amended invocation, now not to be regarded as in any way effecting consecration, is surely evidence of a thinking far more muddled than anything in the *Alternative Form*.

The year after the bishops' compromise and the publication of the Natal rite, 1922, seems to have been, liturgically speaking, a quiet one, partly owing, perhaps, to the fact that it was also the year in which Darragh died. The correspondence columns of the *Church Chronicle* were freer from reference to revision than at any time since the end of the war. Yet when episcopal synod met on 13 November 1922 it almost incredibly attempted a further revision of the pro-anaphora of the rite. The form that this revision took shows the influence of the Pretoria and Natal draft

[1] *Considerations*, p. 8.

rites. The first Lord's prayer was omitted, and was replaced by an invocation of the Trinity and the antiphon to Psalm xliii (but, curiously, not the psalm itself). Proper offertory sentences for use at the greater festivals, and an offertory prayer, were provided. This prayer now appears in the final version of the rite, and it has a curious history. Ultimately it derives from the English coronation service and the Sarum *Missa pro rege*. Gould had advocated that it should be adopted as early as 1918.[2] A version of it was included in the Natal rite, and from there it found its way into the final form. A copy of the 1922 edition of the *Alternative Form*, preserved in the files of the bishops of Kimberley, is interesting on this point. The prayer is written into the printed form of the service in pencil, presumably by Bishop Gore Browne who was bishop of Kimberley at the time. Bishop Gore Browne wrote the prayer first in one form, and later corrected it to another, as though the wording were being worked over in synod. If this is what the pencilled note means, it shows that members of episcopal synod as a whole (for the bishop was not a member of the liturgical committee) took an active part in the details of revision.

Various changes were also made in the prayer for the Church and the present versicle and response were inserted before the prayer of Thanksgiving. These were taken from the Revised Prayer Book (Permissive Use) Measure of 1923, or, more probably, from its source in the 'Orange Book'.[3] They did not appear in the English Revised Book of 1928. Extra post-communion collects and several new prefaces were also added to the *Alternative Form* of 1923. The only changes in the anaphora were the insertion of 'indeed' after 'All Glory and Thanksgiving' and the transference of the word 'made' from after the bracketed phrase in the first paragraph to before it. Both these changes were rescinded again in the following year. The 1923 edition seems to have been purely experimental. It was described as 'faddist' by one critic, and a great many of the changes proposed in it were abandoned for the final edition in 1924.

Phelps, as convener of the liturgical committee, published a schedule of the chief of these alterations early in 1923. He also reported that a copy of the newly revised experimental edition was to be sent to the committee of liturgical experts appointed by

---

[2] *Church Chronicle*, xv, p. 269.
[3] *Proposals for the Alternative Prayer Book* (Alcuin Club, 1923), pt. I, p. 51.

the archbishop of Canterbury in terms of the resolution of the
Lambeth conference of 1920. The committee was to be asked its
opinion of the rite as a whole and also on certain particular points,
the translation of the *Gloria in excelsis*, the method of consecration,
and the position of the fraction. The Natal rite had made provision
for the 'greater fraction' either during the prayer of Oblation,
immediately after the words 'bounden duty and service', or at the
end of the Lord's prayer. None of the official revisions up to and
including 1922 had made any provision for a fraction (other than
the 'breaking' directed among the manual acts). In 1923 the
words 'Then shall the Priest break the bread and . . .' were added
to the rubric immediately after the prayer of Humble Access.

It has already been noted that episcopal synod had resolved to
send a copy of the 1922 edition to the archbishop of Canterbury's
'Lambeth' committee. At the time the South African liturgical
committee had recommended

seeking advice from the Liturgical Committee appointed by the
Archbishop of Canterbury, with regard to the Form as a whole,
together with such questions as:
  (1) The Decalogue of [sc. or] the Gospel Summary of the Law
  (2) Seasonal sentences at the Offertory
  (3) Prayer at the offering of the bread and wine
  (4) Addition[al] of a Memorial of Creation to the invariable Preface
  (5) A Fraction at the Our Father
  (6) The rubric governing a further Consecration where necessary
  (7) Addition of a Prayer to the Holy Trinity before the Blessing[4]

Bazeley had advocated the seeking of such advice as early as
March 1921, when he wrote that it was to be hoped that 'the
Archbishop's committee will tell us what is most important, what
is less important, and what is positively undesirable'.[5] Yet, in
spite of the resolutions of episcopal synod, there is no clear
evidence that either the 1922 or the 1923 edition of the *Alternative
Form* was ever sent to the 'Lambeth' committee. And if either was
sent, there is no evidence that the committee ever gave an answer.
Frere quite clearly thought, in December 1922 (when there would
have been a whole year for the first resolution of the episcopal
synod to have been put into effect) that the South African rite had
never been submitted to the 'Lambeth' committee.[6] At that date

[4] *Church Chronicle*, XVIII, p. 396.
[5] *Theology*, II, p. 162.
[6] Cf. Jasper, *Walter Howard Frere*, p. 235.

there would not have been time for the edition of 1923 (that is, the rite as amended by episcopal synod in November 1922) to have been sent to England, and it is just possible that the earlier edition was kept back till it could be sent with the later one. It would certainly be extraordinary if the bishops' resolutions had never been carried out at all; yet it is quite clear that, whether Phelps sent the copies to England or not, no reply reached this country before the liturgy was approved by provincial synod in 1924. Less than a year elapsed between the printing of the 1923 edition and the final revision of the *Alternative Form*. No record of any reply from the archbishop of Canterbury's committee is to be found in the minutes of the one session of the episcopal synod which took place in the interval. Nor has any answer been kept among the papers of the liturgical committee. Such an important document was almost bound to leave some trace. It is just possible that a reply was received at a much later date; if so, and it does not seem likely, it can have had no effect upon the South African rite.

The episcopal synod met to review the form for the last time early in November 1923. They rescinded a good many of the experimental amendments made in the previous year. It seems extraordinary that, when the form had received widespread support after the compromise on the invocation, the bishops should have embarked upon the edition of 1923 at all. Probably they were anxious that it should not be said that they had ignored the suggestions made in the Natal and Pretoria draft rites. Probably the bishops were not wholehearted in desiring the sort of amendments proposed in 1923, and certainly the more radical of those amendments were unacceptable in the Province. The omission of the first Lord's prayer, for instance, seems to have been altogether too blatant a break with Anglican tradition. It was restored in the final form and so, with some additions from the 'Grey Book',[7] was the 1919 version of the prayer for the Church. The offertory prayer, the seasonal offertory sentences, the second fraction, and the versicle and response after the Communion, were the features of the experimental edition of 1923 which were retained in the final form. Such slight changes as had been made in the anaphora for 1923 were rescinded again for 1924, and the

---

[7] *Church Chronicle*, xxi, p. 756. The 'Grey Book' was *A New Prayer Book*, with a foreword by Bishop W. Temple (Oxford University Press, 1923).

bishops' preface was reprinted unaltered in the final edition of the *Alternative Form*.

The next move in the ratification of the liturgy lay with the provincial registrar, who towards the end of 1924 published a solemn and official definition of the canonical powers of provincial synod in matters of revision, and gave warning that if synod passed the new rite it would become a part of Church law and would have to be observed by the clergy under their oath of obedience and their declarations. Synod met in November. Phelps, still bishop of Grahamstown, 'moved in a most lucid speech that a general consent be given to the Alternative Form. . . . After a full discussion this was agreed to with only one dissentient.'[8] At this point a Natal clergyman moved a resolution expressing loyalty to the 1662 rite. This was also passed by synod. For at any rate the next five years, the form was official and could not be altered. In 1929 provincial synod again approved the *Alternative Form*, this time without there being any need for discussion at all.[9] As it had now been passed by two successive sessions the form could only have been further amended by opening the whole process again *de novo*. The liturgy was fixed.

It had been arrived at by a long series of compromises. There had been the basic compromise between the theology of consecration as advocated by Bazeley and Gould, and the language suggested by Frere. Conservative opinion had been satisfied by making the new rite a secondary alternative to 1662. The Westernizers had been far more difficult to placate and their intransigence had led to the excision of the controversial phrases from the invocation, and the inclusion of the 1662 form for supplementary consecration as an alternative to the form laid down in 1919. But none of these diplomatic manoeuvrings had in the least affected the official interpretation placed upon the new rite by the bishops. Even after the final compromise of 1921 they continued to assert in their preface that the theme of the consecration prayer was Thanksgiving. There is no mention in the preface of invocation and but little of the narrative of the Institution. Thanksgiving is the central and consecratory idea. However much the details of the language may have been shaped by compromise the bishops consistently maintained that consecration was effected by Thanksgiving. In 1921 they were still thinking in terms of the anaphora as a series of thanksgivings, since they planned to ask the 'Lambeth' committee for advice on a memorial of creation. Neither Frere's influence nor the petitions from the clergy altered this official interpretation of the theology of the form.

The interpretation was official. Even though the preface was drafted by Phelps in the first place, it was not his work alone. The liturgical committee saw his draft, and at least one of the members, Bishop Baines, made alterations to it. Episcopal synod adopted the preface and caused it to be reprinted in the editions of 1920, 1922, and 1924. That they did so deliberately, and not carelessly or by accident, may be proved by reference to their statement on the compromise over the invocation, in which they formally resolved that they believed consecration to be effected by thanksgiving and not by any particular part of the consecration prayer. The bishops were not only the revisers of the rite, they were responsible for the authoritative publication of it. And when they had published it, provincial synod gave its sanction to their form. The bishops' preface was printed in the edition of the rite provincial synod confirmed in 1924 and 1929—and synod passed the rite 'as printed'. The idea in the mind of W. C. Bishop and expressed in an obscure article in the *Church Quarterly Review* half a century ago, became the mind, not only of the framers of the rite, but of the bishops who 'set it forth', and of the Province which sanctioned it.

The rite is accused of being muddled in its form of consecration. But this objection is only valid if one holds that the rite possesses, what the bishops maintained that it did not possess, a moment of consecration. There can be no objection to two invocations unless one believes that consecration is effected by one of them alone. There can be no objection to the language of the second invocation unless one believes that consecration is completed by the words of Institution alone, or by those words and the first invocation. If one is prepared to leave aside the idea of a 'moment of consecration', then those things which might seem muddled, unnecessary, or untheological are seen to express a very clear theology—a theology which held that 'when thanksgiving has been offered in prayerful trust that God's power will accomplish his purpose, we then can securely believe in the Presence of Our Lord in the Eucharist . . .'.

Not all liturgical scholars have felt that the South African rite is muddled and obscure. Srawley, while obviously unhappy about the two invocations, is much more cautious than some South African critics have been, and draws a parallel on this point with some of the Mozarabic masses.[10] Canon Lowther Clarke's views are similar to those of the South African bishops. 'For myself', he wrote, 'I prefer the view that the Prayer of Consecration as a whole effects Consecration.'[11] Holding this view, he goes on to say:

But I see the force of the objection that since 1552 Consecration has been identified in English minds with the Words of Institution, and that to throw doubt on this is most disturbing. Those who lament the maimed Canon of 1662 ought not to be told that they must continue as they are or else accept what seems to them an Eastern view of Consecration. The modification which would unite the Anglican Communion most would be one on American or South African lines.

After commenting briefly on the American form of the invocation and claiming that the South African form is even better, Lowther Clarke continues:

The difficulty about the form of reconsecration would then disappear; but to obviate all possible scruples it would be well to add a rubric that it is sufficient to use the 1662 words.

These comments show that a scholar holding the same theology of consecration as the South African bishops arrived at the same solution of the problem. In the article from which these extracts have been quoted Lowther Clarke was attempting to find some way of expressing his own theology without alienating those who held a rather different view. This is exactly the same problem as the South African bishops had to face. Lowther Clarke's solution is to adopt a form such as the bishops adopted in this country, even in the case of a second consecration. This suggests that the rite devised by the South African bishops is not the result of compromise for the sake of compromise but is exactly the form likely to be framed by those who hold a definite and clear theology of a particular kind, when faced with particular problems.

Two points only might be used to argue that the bishops were not framing the rite upon the theology which has been attributed

[10] *Liturgy and Worship* (S.P.C.K., 1932), p. 348.
[11] Article in Theology Reprints, No. 12, *The 1549 Canon* (reprinted from *Theology* for February 1933), p. 11.

to them: the rubrics directing the manual acts, and the rubric on supplementary consecration. Both these two points might conceivably be used to show that the South African rite was to be interpreted in terms of a 'Western' theology of consecration. (Since the compromise of 1921 no one could maintain that the rite was Eastern in this respect.) But we have already seen that the rubrics directing the manual acts are unsatisfactory evidence for proving anything, and Lowther Clarke's remarks suggest that, if anything, the rubric on supplementary consecration proves that the bishops held neither the Eastern nor the Western view of consecration. It is interesting to note that he advocated adopting 'a rubric that it is *sufficient to use the 1662 words*', for this is exactly what the South African bishops had done. They directed that the priest was either to use the whole consecration prayer again from the beginning of the first invocation to the end of the second, or to use the 'Form provided for this purpose in the Book of Common Prayer'. It is to be noted that, although the bishops are at pains to copy out the exact words to be used in the first case, they do not do so in the second. When in 1918 the bishops simply wished to use the *words* of 1662, they copied the rubric exactly. But the alternative form for supplementary consecration in the South African rite is specifically not this or that form of words singled out from that rite but *the form used in the rite of 1662*. It is not the words used, as such, which matter. The words are in the South African rite still, yet they are not referred to except under the title of the first official rite of the Province—the rite of 1662. What the rubric says, in effect, is, 'or you may use the form for supplementary consecration from our other Prayer Book'. No doubt this alternative was inserted in tenderness to 'those who find in the recital of the words of institution the central moment of the service',[12] and for the convenience of busy priests with large numbers of communicants, yet the way in which the rubric has been phrased makes it evident that the bishops were not muddling but were making a concession which did not conflict with their clear and coherent theology. The rubric is simply an extension of the principle recognized throughout revision that the rite of 1662 is 'a sufficient and completely catholic rite' and that the two Prayer Books are alternative, not exclusive or contradictory; though it is also an exception to the other fundamental principle

---

[12] Gould in *Church Chronicle*, XXI, p. 756; and cf. Lowther Clarke, p. 12.

that the rites of the two books must not be intermingled but each must be used in its entirety.

It is not the purpose of this study to examine the rationale of the consecration prayer of 1662. It is with the *fact* of that rite that we are concerned, a rite which is canonical and which is in use in this Province. Our concern is to interpret the meaning of the *Alternative Form*, and that can only be done in terms of the expressed intentions of the men who framed it, of the bishops who issued it, and of the Province which sanctioned and uses it. The rubric on supplementary consecration does not contradict, but, properly understood, confirms their expressed intentions.

The bishops' theology of consecration was that the whole of the Great Thanksgiving is the consecratory 'form'. So far as it is possible to show what their eucharistic doctrine in a wider sense was, this, too, can be seen to presuppose such a theology of consecration. The bishops regarded the idea of 'offering' or 'sacrifice' as the central theme in all eucharistic theology. Twice in the short preface to the *Alternative Form* they expound the meaning of the rite in terms of offering. Set out consecutively, these parts of the preface give a brief but adequate exposition of the rite, and an exposition which makes it clear how central was the belief that consecration is effected by thanksgiving.

It is important to bring out the fact that the Service of the Holy Communion is the great Thanksgiving or Eucharist of the Church. In the four accounts of the Institution the giving of thanks by Our Lord is as important a feature as the breaking of the bread or the words of administration. The Services which have come down to us from the early centuries of Christianity, as well as those in use in the Churches of our Communion in America and Scotland, show by their structure that, if the example of Our Lord is to be followed and we are to 'Do this in remembrance of' Him, the note of Thanksgiving must be sounded more clearly than in the Book of 1661 (our present Book).

This note of Thanksgiving has always been represented in Christian Liturgies by the Preface . . . leading up to the Sanctus. . . . But in our Service after that point this note is not heard again till after the Communion, whereas in the older Services the chief facts of Our Lord's Life and Work are made the subject of Thanksgiving.

In this revised Service the whole of the central portion from the Preface to the Lord's Prayer has been, by some very few alterations, thrown into a definitely eucharistic form.

This revision of the Service in the direction of more definite thanksgiving, helps to bring out the fact that the Eucharist has a Godward side as being the offering to God of a corporate act of worship and praise. The Archbishops of Canterbury and York in their reply (1897) to the attack made by the Pope on our status as a Church, emphasized this fact. Thanksgiving lifts us up in thought to God in Heaven, where the whole Church offers its worship continually. The present revision concentrates attention more upon the heavenly sphere where the worship of God is accomplished, than upon the earthly altar which is the symbol of the true, and the offering made in the Eucharist is seen to be that of the whole Church and not simply of the Celebrant.

At the same time the necessity of personal devotion and the reality of the personal gift in the Sacrament of the Holy Communion are maintained unimpaired. . . .

Thus the order of thought in the revised Service is as follows:

First by Confession and Absolution the congregation is prepared for the supreme act of worship.

Then, in the Preface, Sanctus and Prayer of Consecration, no longer interrupted by the Prayer of Humble Access, we lift up our hearts in an unbroken act of Praise and Thanksgiving.

And having completed this offering with the Lord's Prayer, we then prepare ourselves for the reception of the Holy Gifts by acknowledging our unworthiness and praying that our communion may be for the benefit of our bodies and souls. . . .

In the Prayer for the Church Militant . . . we are reminded that we approach God's throne not as individuals but as members of the mystical Body of Christ Our Lord. . . .

The reunion of the Prayer of Oblation with the Prayer of Consecration, followed by the Our Father makes it clearer:

(a) that we must first present Christ and His merits before God as the justification for our approach,

(b) that we then present ourselves trusting in the merits of our Head,

(c) that having been thus lifted up into the heavenly sphere we can say the Prayer that Christ taught us,

(d) and last, because greatest privilege of all, receive Him Who is our Life.

The Lord's Prayer is the greatest of all prayers, and contains in itself Worship, Intercession, Petition, Penitence, and Praise. It is therefore specially suitable as the conclusion of the solemn Prayer of Consecration, for it gathers up, in the highest form, all that has been prayed for therein.

The train of thought in the bishops' minds seems to have been somewhat as follows:

The principal theme of the whole eucharist is corporate 'offering' or 'sacrifice'.

In the Anglican Church the eucharistic sacrifice is thought of as one of praise and thanksgiving.

But offering or sacrifice is not to be divorced from consecration —offering and consecration are identical.

Therefore consecration (like the offering) must be one of praise and thanksgiving.

So the whole of the bishops' eucharistic theology led logically to the belief that consecration is effected by a prayer of Thanksgivings.

It is interesting to note that the recent report of the Church of England Liturgical Commission has listed a number of new trends in eucharistic scholarship which have led them to desire a rather different approach to revision than was adopted in 1927/8. Among these trends much emphasis is laid upon the fact that:

We know now, in a way that was not realised in 1928, that the Eucharist has developed directly out of Jewish forms of thanksgiving, that the first Christians thought of consecration as effected by thanksgiving, and that the controversies between Eastern and Western views of consecration . . . belong to a later, not to the earliest period.[13]

The next two trends listed are, a new approach to the idea of eucharistic sacrifice, and the recovered emphasis on the corporate nature of the eucharist—the very ideas which are to be found linked with Thanksgiving in the South African bishops' preface to the *Alternative Form*. Thirty years ago, when these ideas had not been so generally recognized as they are now, the bishops deliberately set out to fashion the rite round them. These are now the very ideas which it is thought desirable for any Anglican liturgy to express. It may be argued that the South African rite does not express them very well—less well, perhaps, than they were expressed in the anaphora of Bazeley and Gould's *Proposals*. But the bishops were restrained by the emphasis which the Lambeth conferences and the constitution of the Province alike had laid upon the Prayer Book as a source of unity throughout the Anglican Communion.[14] The preface to the *Alternative Form* ends with the words:

[13] *Prayer Book Revision in the Church of England* (S.P.C.K., 1957), pp. 21 f.

[14] *Constitution and Canons* (1950), Article I (pp. 7 f.), the second proviso (p. 8), and Article X (p. 12); and cf. *Prayer Book Revision in the Church of England*, pp. 29 f., 35, 42 ff.

With regard to the doctrine underlying this revised Service the Bishops are confident that it adheres, with the utmost loyalty, to 'The Faith of our Lord Jesus Christ, as taught in the Holy Scriptures, held by the Primitive Church, summed up in the Creeds, and affirmed by the undisputed General Councils' (Article I of the Constitution).

Article I of the constitution also says:

The Province . . . receives the Book of Common Prayer . . . to be used, according to the form therein prescribed, in Public Prayer and Administration of the Sacraments and other Holy Offices . . . and, further, disclaims for itself the right of altering any of the aforesaid Standards. . . .

The South African revisers *could* only give expression to their theology of consecration and of the eucharist within the framework of the Book of Common Prayer and without departing from its standards.

The Present State of the Documentary Evidence

IT APPEARS that Canon Gould intended, in the 1940's, to write a complete history of the South African Prayer Book. Unfortunately he died before he could achieve this aim, and no manuscript has survived amongst his papers. In the course of collecting the material for this projected work Gould wrote two letters to Mrs. Bazeley, the widow of his former colleague.[1] These letters are valuable evidence and indicate the fate of a good deal of the relevant documents. Mrs. Bazeley had sent Gould such of her husband's papers as still existed. Gould's own papers had been destroyed some time previously. The papers from Mrs. Bazeley included some written by Dr. Darragh and a nearly complete set of the various editions of the South African rite. In 1942 Gould sent some of the papers he had collected to the Central Church Record Library, housed at the University of the Witwatersrand, and others to the South African Public Library in Cape Town, where they may still be found. The present Bishop of Mashonaland, the Rt. Rev. C. W. Alderson, who was warden of St. Paul's College from 1938 to 1943, recollects that Gould wrote to him at the time offering him some liturgical papers for the college library. The only trace of this transaction now to be found in the college is the collection of books inscribed as having been used by Bazeley in the preparation of the South African liturgy.[2]

In the second of his letters to Mrs. Bazeley (dated 23 September 1942) Gould described his attempts to locate further material. What he then wrote agrees almost exactly with the findings of the present writer, whose search for material had been virtually completed by the time these two letters of Canon Gould's came to light.

Canon Gould wrote:

The Bishop of Kimberley has been secretary of the Liturgical Committee ever since he took over from Francis Phelps when the latter became

[1] These letters are now in St. Paul's College library.
[2] This inscription is for many reasons unreliable.

Archbishop. (*That was in 1931. The Bishop of Kimberley was Theodore Gibson, subsequently bishop of St. John's. He continued as secretary and later as convener of the committee until his resignation in 1950.*) From what Mrs. Phelps tells me it seems that F.R.P. destroyed practically all his liturgical papers before he left Grahamstown in 1931; anyway he handed none worth speaking of to the Bp. of Kimberley. (*For a list of what has been preserved by the liturgical committee see the latter part of this appendix. Bishop Fisher, convener of the committee in succession to Phelps, recalls that no minutes were kept until Bishop Gibson became secretary and that Phelps used to note amendments in an interleaved copy of the South African rite.*) And he left none at Bishopsbourne. (*Bishopsbourne is the residence of the bishops of Grahamstown. The present bishop, the Rt. Rev. A. H. Cullen, D.D., who succeeded Phelps, confirms that his predecessor left no liturgical papers among his files.*) Nor did he give any to Father Victor, (*Fr. Osmund Victor, C.R., was, at the time when Gould wrote, provincial archivist, in charge of the Central Church Record Library.*) nor are there any at Bishopscourt, (*Bishopscourt is the residence of the archbishops of Cape Town. The Rev. C. T. Wood, domestic chaplain to Archbishop Phelps, devoted a good deal of his time and attention to ordering the records kept at Bishopscourt. He confirms that there were no liturgical papers among these records. There is nothing relevant at Bishopscourt now except the minutes of the episcopal synod.*) or the Provincial Office. (*The only papers having a bearing on liturgical revision now to be found in the provincial secretary's office in Church House in Cape Town are the proof sheets sent out from England when the complete Prayer Book was first published by the Oxford University Press after the provincial synod in 1950.*) The three bishops most active in the early stages of revision were Chandler (*of Bloemfontein, 1902-20*), Williams of St. John's and Bp. Nash (*C.R., coadjutor bishop of Cape Town*). So I wrote to Archdeacon Clarke, Chandler's biographer, to Williams's executor, and Bp. Nash at Mirfield. The first had found nothing about the S.A. Liturgy in all the papers he went through, and the two others had destroyed them all. But at Kimberley there was a file of Bp. Gore-Browne's, who was not on the Liturgical Committee, but who had kept some—at all events—of the papers he had received as a member of Episcopal Synod: and that was a really useful find. (*These papers still exist in the files of the bishops of Kimberley. They were used by the present Bishop of George, the Rt. Rev. J. Hunter, when he was at Kimberley, for a paper on the South African rite. It was through him that the present writer learnt of their existence. At George, itself, as in most other dioceses, none of the early liturgical papers have been preserved.*)

In addition to the various sources mentioned by Gould in the letter quoted above, there are the records of the liturgical committee, now housed in the diocesan library in Cape Town. No minutes were kept until 1931; and none of the correspondence and only a few of the more obviously important papers were preserved before that date. After 1931, when the liturgy had already received final ratification from provincial synod, everything seems to have been kept, including letters from persons who were quite obviously mentally unbalanced. Amongst this very complete collection is another letter from Gould, dated 20 December 1941, in which he complains to the secretary of the committee that he has been unable to find any liturgical papers for the period 1917/24 at Bishopscourt in Cape Town. This letter belongs to the same period as Gould's letters to Mrs. Bazeley and was written in the course of his search for material for a history of the rite.

The material kept at the Central Church Record Library consists chiefly of the pamphlets sent there by Gould in 1942. This is true also of the documents in the South African Public Library.

The minutes of the episcopal synod, kept at Bishopscourt, are, where relevant at all, chiefly a formal list of resolutions proposed, adopted, or rejected, on the recommendation of the liturgical committee. As the minutes often refer simply to the numbers of the paragraphs in the committee's reports and as not all these reports now exist, it is not always possible to determine exactly what episcopal synod did decide except by reference to the printed editions of the rite issued after the session of the synod. This means that one can always discover what went into the rite, but not always what was rejected. Only constant reference to the reports would make it possible to interpret the minutes exactly, and the matter is further complicated by the fact that, whereas the minutes are kept at the archbishop's home, the reports, where these exist at all, are sometimes to be found only in a place some hundreds of miles away. Continual cross-reference and comparison is impossible. The proceedings of episcopal synod, moreover, are never made public (except for brief statements issued occasionally by the synod) and the minutes could not, of course, be removed from Bishopscourt. Indeed, it was only through the kindness of the late archbishop, the Most Rev. Dr. Geoffrey Clayton, that this source of information was made available at all.

Some of the papers from the diocese of St. Johns have been preserved by the Rev. G. Bacon, rector of Maclear. The most valuable of these is a copy of the paper read to the Society of Sacred Study in that diocese by Canon Mason.

Another valuable source of information is the Rev. R. C. D. Jasper's published collection of the liturgical papers of Bishop Frere. Both Mr. Jasper and Fr. Bernard Horner, C.R., Frere's literary executor, assure me that all the papers left by the bishop which have a bearing on the South African rite were included in that collection.

In the absence of any correspondence addressed to the liturgical committee during the years in which the eucharistic liturgy was framed, the correspondence columns of the *Church Chronicle*, then the official journal of the Province, have proved invaluable. A full set of the bound volumes of this magazine are kept in the diocesan library in Cape Town. Volume XXI (1924) of the series contains an article by Canon Gould entitled 'The South African Liturgy', a very short but illuminating account of revision up to 1924. Gould's account needs some correction in matters of detail which have been noted in the body of this study, but the main outline is reliable. The article was written just before the present South African rite was presented to provincial synod for the first time.

Also by Gould, but of less value for this study, is a chapter in *Historical Records* on the episcopate of Bishop Phelps, which refers in part to the beginnings of revision in this country. Another chapter of *Historical Records* is avowedly devoted to the South African liturgy, but it is very brief and consists chiefly of two extracts from *The Kingdom*, the magazine of the diocese of Pretoria. Some not very detailed information may also be found in *Liturgy and Worship*.[3]

[3] Ed. W. K. Lowther Clarke (S.P.C.K., 1932).

INDEX

Administration of Holy Communion, Alternative Form of the Order for the; see Alternative Form
Administration, Words of, 21, 27, 31, 72
Agnus Dei, 38, 96
Alston, W. T., 37 f., 78
Alternative Form, 1919, 31, 36, 51, 53, 56, 62, 64, 68 f., 85, 97, 102, 104
—— 1920, 71 ff., 78 f., 91, 94 f., 97, 102, 110
—— 1922, 100 f., 107, 110
—— 1923, 106 ff.
—— 1924, 108 f., 110
Alternative Liturgy, An, See Rite, Natal Draft
Ambrose, 23 n., 79
Ambrose, Pseudo-, 23 n., 79
Anaphora (Consecration Prayer, Canon), 5, 9 f., 18 ff., 34, 38 ff., 42 f., 47 ff., 54, 60, 70 f., 72, 75, 80, 87, 95, 99 f., 101, 103 f., 108, 111
Anderson, T. J., 36
Apostolic Constitutions, Book VIII (A.C. VIII), 19 ff., 26
Assessors to Liturgical Committee; see Liturgical Committee
Athanasius, 23 n.

Baines, F. S., bishop of Natal, 31, 58, 60, 76, 110
Bazeley, J. S., 11 f., 17 ff., 33 f., 37, 43, 49 f., 57, 61, 65, 69 f., 75, 101, 107, 109, 115, 117
Benedictus Qui Venit, 22, 41, 52, 58 f., 95, 102
Bishop, W. C., 17 ff., 24, 34, 41, 58, 83 n., 88, 110
Brightman, F. E., 27, 84, 88 f.
Browne, W. Gore, bishop of Kimberley, 106, 118
Bull, H. P., 94, 96

Canon of the Mass; see Anaphora
Carter, W. M., archbishop of Cape Town, 44 f., 68
Chandler, A., bishop of Bloemfontein, 40, 66, 118
Chapters, Diocesan, 44, 47, 54 f.
Chrysostom, 12, 23 n.
—— Liturgy of St.; see Liturgy
Church Chronicle, The, 35, 37, 66, 74, 77 f., 91 f., 120

Church Quarterly Review, The (C.Q.R.) 54, 59. 110
Cirlot, F, L., 19, 81
Clarke, W. K. Lowther, 111 f., 120 n,
Clement, 20
Colenso, J. W., bishop of Natal, 1 ff.
Comfortable Words, 5
Commandments (Decalogue), 4, 47, 73
Commission, The Church of England Liturgical, 115 f.
Committee on Liturgical Questions, The Church of England Advisory; see Liturgical Questions
Committee, The Lambeth Liturgical; see Liturgical Committee, Lambeth
Committee, The South African Liturgical, on Prayer Book Revision and Adaptation, etc.; see Liturgical Committee
Common Prayer, Book of; see Prayer Book
Consecration, Form of, 27, 38, 60 f., 63 f., 75 ff., 82, 86 ff., 91 ff., 97, 99, 104, 109 ff., 112 f.
—— Prayer; see Anaphora
Considerations Bearing on the Petition to Episcopal Synod, 64, 77 f., 84 f., 90 f., 94, 104
Constitution of the Province, 1 ff., 44, 115
Constitutions, Apostolic; see Apostolic Constitutions
Convocations, of Canterbury and York, 3 f., 15, 42, 44, 54, 73
Cornish, C. E., bishop of Grahamstown, 12, 39
Cosin, Bishop, 42
Cranmer, Archbishop, 23, 63, 105
Cyril of Jerusalem, 12, 23 n.

Darragh, J. T., 64 f., 75 ff., 80 ff., 87 ff. 92 ff., 97, 100, 102, 104, 117
Dearmer, Percy, 11, 84, 86
Decalogue; see Commandments
Deir Balizeh papyri, 18
Dix, G., 19
Duchesne, L., 21, 23
Dutch Reformed Church, 1

Epiklesis; see Invocation
Episcopal Synod; see Synod

121